This book is to be returned on or before the date above.
It may be borrowed for a further period if not in demand.

Essex County Council
Libraries

HANBURY PLAYS

**KEEPER'S LODGE
BROUGHTON GREEN
DROITWICH
WORCESTERSHIRE WR9 7EE**

BY THE SAME AUTHOR

ROSMERSHOLM (in a new English version)
SWEENEY TODD THE BARBER
LADY AUDLEY'S SECRET or DEATH IN LIME TREE WALK
THREE HISSES FOR VILLAINY!!! (three one-act melodramas)
THE DRUNKARD or DOWN WITH DEMON DRINK!
BEING OF SOUND MIND
A TALE OF TWO CITIES (adapted from Charles Dickens)
PRIDE AND PREJUDICE (adapted from Jane Austen)
MURDER PLAY
DRINK TO ME ONLY
THE LAST LAUGH
FROM THREE TO FOUR
FACE THE QUEEN
THE FINAL MOVEMENT
A QUESTION OF PROFIT
HE AND SHE (three one-act duologues)
TEA WITH JASON
SUDDEN DEATH
GHOST OF A CHANCE
EAST LYNNE or NEVER CALLED ME MOTHER!
DEATH MASQUE
CHEERS, TEARS AND SCREAMERS! (three mini melodramas)
FOILED AGAIN! (three more mini melodramas)
THE WOODPILE
VISITING TIME
NINE WOMEN - NO MEN
LINES OF COMMUNICATION (15 duologues)
A BEAR WITH A SORE HEAD (adapted from Chekov)
LADIES ONLY 1 (four sketches for women)
LADIES ONLY 4 (four more sketches for women)
WILL POWER (A one-man show)

First published 1964
This edition first published 1987

© Brian J. Burton 1964 1987
ISBN: 185205 049 7

PERFORMING RIGHTS

PERFORMING RIGHTS

Applications should be made as follows:-

U.K. - Samuel French Ltd 52 Fitzroy Street London W1P 6JR

U.S.A. - Samuel French Inc. 45 West 25th St, New York 10010

CANADA :- Samuel French (Canada) Ltd, 80 Richmond Street East
Toronto, Ontario M5 1PC

AUSTRALIA:- Dominie Pty, 8 Cross St, Brookvale N.S.W. 2100

NEW ZEALAND:- Play Bureau (NZ) Ltd P.O. Box 420, New Plymouth

SOUTH AFRICA (Transvaal) D.A.L. R. O. (Pty) Ltd P.O. Box 9292, 2000 Johannesburg

SOUTH AFRICA (except Transvaal) Miss A.C. Grace, "Eureka" Sherard Square
Wynberg CP7800

EAST AFRICA:- Phoenix Players Ltd P.O. Box 52383, Nairobi, Kenya

ZIMBABWE: - National Theatre Organisation, P.O. Box 2701, Harare

IRELAND: - Thomas J. Mooney 282 Swords Road Dublin 9

MALTA:- Benedict H. Dingli Esq. Dingli International Ltd,
43/4 Zacharay St Valetta

All other countries :- Samuel French, London

THE MURDER OF MARIA MARTEN or THE RED BARN

was first presented, in this revised version, at the SWAN THEATRE,
Worcester, on December 6th, 1978, with the following cast:-

William Corder	Peter Jones
Thomas Marten	Keith Bridgwater
Tim Bobbin	Larry Collins
Johnny Badger	Andrew Leggott
Maria Marten	Chris Carmichael
Mrs Marten	Gabrielle Bullock
Anne Marten	Judy Armitage
Meg Bobbin	Suzanne Ranford
Nell Hatfield	Honor Moody
Petra Andrews	Anne Tithecott
Carmen James	Joy Hancock
Rosa Post	Jean Small
Alice Rumble	Susan Hopkins
Pharos Lee	Andrew Leggott

Directed by	Brian J. Burton
Designer	John Cartwright
Musical direction.	Judith Holden
Stage Manager	Jeanne Bryson
Lighting	Ray Gravenall
Costumes	Winifred Gardner and Jane Hale
Drums	Paul Daniels

III

To
My very dear New Zealand friends
STAN and BETTY CAMPBELL

INTRODUCTION

In all the main essentials, this is a true story. Maria Marten was born in Polstead, Suffolk in 1801. There she met William Corder, by whom she had a child who died in infancy. In 1827, Corder murdered Maria and buried her body in the Red Barn. Because of his wife's recurring dream, Thomas Marten searched the barn and discovered the body of his daughter. Corder was arrested in London, where he had married. He was tried and convicted of the crime and in 1828 was executed at Bury Goal.

There have been many plays written on the subject; indeed at Polstead Fair, held a month before the trial of Corder, two plays were produced based on THE LATE MURDER OF MARIA MARTEN. By the end of that year, a number of theatres were presenting melodramas based on the murder. At Weymouth, playgoers were thrilled with a lurid version called THE RED BARN or THE GYPSY'S CURSE and, in London, two versions ran simultaneously. These were ADVERTISEMENT FOR WIVES and THE RED BARN or THE MYSTERIOUS MURDER. Another early playbill includes a version, presented at the theatre in Lincoln, on October 27th, 1830, entitled RED BARN or THE PROPHETIC DREAM - a new melodrama in four acts, founded on fact. The playbill informed its readers that the piece had been 'brought forward, not only from the unprecedented success it has been received with at the various theatres in the kingdom, but as a moral lesson, that murder, however for the time concealed, will speak with most miraculous organ.'

The first printed version was that performed at the Star Theatre, Swansea, in 1842, and was called MARIA MARTIN (Note the spelling of the surname) or THE MURDER IN THE RED BARN. This was quite short and shared the bill with other plays. Another, described as a traditional acting version was published in 1928. This was the Queen's Theatre, Battersea version edited by Montagu Slater.

In 1927, Tod Slaughter presented MARIA MARTEN at the old Elephant Theatre, where it played to packed houses for five months. Other versions have been filmed, broadcast and televised. In addition, there have been a number of novels based on the story - one of which, published over a hundred years ago, has provided some of the material for this new version.

Unlike any other published version, this is a full length play and has been designed to be presented in very simple settings with a reasonably small cast. The music and songs have been written for this version but the words of 'The Ballad of William Corder' have been adapted from a contemporary ballad.

A one-act melodrama, THE GYPSY CURSE or THE FLOWER OF THE TRIBE, tells the story of William Corder and the gypsy girl, Zella. This is available from HANBURY PLAYS who also publish the full piano score of THE MURDER OF MARIA MARTEN or THE RED BARN.

Brian J. Burton

(Permission is not required to reprint this introduction in full or in part but acknowledgment should be made)

CHARACTERS IN THE PLAY

William Corder - the Squire's son
Thomas Marten - an honest rustic in the vale of years
Tim Bobbin - a simple rustic
Johnny Badger - a young man in love with Maria
Pharos Lee - an officer of the law
Maria Marten - daughter of Thomas Marten
Mrs Marten - wife to Thomas Marten
Anne Marten - his younger daughter
Meg Bobbin - Tim's sister
Nell Hatfield - a gypsy woman
Petra Andrews - a gypsy
Rosa Post - another gypsy
Carmen James - another gypsy
Alice Rumble - Corder's maidservant

SYNOPSIS OF SCENES

PROLOGUE	The auditorium and stage
ACT ONE	
Scene One:	The village green at Polstead, Suffolk - an afternoon in the 1820's
Scene Two:	A path in a nearby wood - later the same day
Scene Three:	The village green - a week later
Scene Four:	The wood - twelve months later
Scene Five:	Interior of a cottage - later the same day
Scene Six:	The wood - later the same day

INTERVAL

ACT TWO	
Scene One:	Interior of Thomas Marten's cottage - a week later
Scene Two:	The wood - thirty minutes later
Scene Three:	Interior of the Red Barn - fifteen minutes later
Scene Four:	Interior of Thomas Marten's cottage - twelve months later
Scene Five:	Interior of the Red Barn - fifteen minutes later
Scene Six:	The wood - a month later
Scene Seven:	Breakfast room in Corder's London home - a week later
Scene Eight:	The condemned cell - several weeks later

The running time of this play (including songs) is two hours and ten minutes (excluding interval)

PROLOGUE

Before the curtain rises, the cast and musicians enter the auditorium from the rear. They carry hand props, a prop basket, manuscripts, hand mirrors, spare costumes, etc. They proceed towards the stage headed by the actor playing Mr. Marten who, for the purpose of the prologue, is the actor manager of a band of strolling players. On their way, the cast exchange remarks between themselves and greet members of the audience.

Mr. Marten goes through the stage curtains, which are then opened revealing the first set, lit only by working lights. The rest of the cast follow him onto the stage and the musicians take up their places.

For a minute or two, the cast unpack the prop basket, practise scales, do handstands, make last minute adjustments to make-up, limber up, etc. Then Mr. Marten claps his hands. He is then covered by a follow-spot, as the house lights go out.

Marten: To your places, please, ladies and gentlemen. *Act One beginners take up their places round the maypole. The others go off stage, taking with them the prop basket, etc.*

Marten: Good evening, ladies and gentlemen, good evening. And now, for your entertainment, education and edification, the (Blank) Theatre Barnstomers present that gripping drama, 'The Murder of Maria Marten' or 'The Red Barn.' We trust that you, our esteemed audience, will participate in the performance by showing your disapproval of the villain's dastardly deeds in an audible manner, by commiserating with the sweet heroine in her hour of trouble and loudly cheering the avengers of justice. However, the management has asked me to state that the casting onto the stage of any soft fruit or decaying vegetable matter will result in the summoning forth of the officers of the law.

Stepping forward and addressing his remarks to the stage electrician.

Are we ready to commence?

All the lights come up to Panto brightness.

To the pianist

Pray, begin.

The pianist strikes up the introduction of the Maypole Song.

Music Cue 1—(The Maypole Song).

1

ACT ONE

SCENE ONE

THE VILLAGE GREEN AT POLSTEAD, SUFFOLK, IN THE 1820'S. *Late Afternoon. Stage Left is the exterior of Thomas Marten's cottage. To the right of the cottage door is a bench on which are seated* MR. AND MRS. MARTEN. *There is a tree right centre with a seat round it. Centre stage is a maypole around which are dancing* MARIA MARTEN, ANNE MARTEN, TIM BOBBIN, MEG BOBBIN AND JOHNNY BADGER.

MAYPOLE SONG
(ALL)

The boys and girls of Polstead are as happy as can be.
The boys and girls of Polstead are all dancing merrily.
Around and round the maypole,
They dance their cares away.
The boys and girls of Polstead are all happy, blithe and gay.

REPEAT

At the end of the dance, the young people break away from the maypole, laughing.

Johnny (*taking* MARIA'S *hand and leading her right*): Come along, Maria, I've had enough dancing for one day. Let me sit down here for a minute or two. I've scarce any breath left in my body. (*Pulls her to seat right where they sit*).

Tim (*putting one arm around* ANNE *and the other around* MEG *left of maypole.* ANNE *on his right*): Dang me, I never felt as happy since the day I was breeched.

Anne (*breaking away right*): Shut thee mouth, fool!

Tim : I ain't no fool, I'll have 'ee know and that be the truth.

2

Anne : What say 'ee, Maria—don't 'ee think Tim Bobbin the greatest fool that ever drew breath?

Maria (*kindly*) : Oh, leave him be, Anne. You are for ever teasing the poor boy. (*Rising*). Come now, Johnny—time for the next dance. Meg, Anne, Tim—are you ready?

Meg (*running to left of maypole*) : Aye, that I be.

Anne (*crossing* MEG, *to pull* TIM *with her to below maypole*) : And we—ain't we Tim?

Maria (*taking* JOHNNY'S *hand*) : Come on, Johnny, the others are waiting.

Johnny : Let's rest awhile Maria. It's pleasant here under the cool shade of this tree.

Maria : Plenty of time for rest later on, Johnny.

Meg: Be 'ee coming, Johnny Badger?

Maria : He's coming (*pulling him up from the seat*) and when we've had but one more dance, then can he rest to his heart's content.

Johnny : Oh, very well—but once more then (*Goes to right of maypole with* MARIA *and they take up their positions. They start to dance*).

Music Cue 2—(Maypole Song Reprise)

Tim (*calling out at top of his voice*) : Oh! Oh! Oh!

The dance ends in confusion.

Meg : What is it?

Anne : What be the matter?

Tim (*to D.S.C. holding his stomach and groaning loudly*) : Oh, dear, Oh Lordy me!

The others crowd round him. MEG *and* ANNE *on his left,* MARIA *and* JOHNNY *on his right.*

Maria : Where's the pain, Tim?

Tim : Here in my stomach. It's rumbling like an old hurdy-gurdy. Oh! Oh!

Anne : Shall I run fetch the doctor, Tim?

Tim (*straightening up*) : It ain't a doctor I be needing.

Meg : What be it then—an undertaker?

Tim : Food! Lots of lovely food. I be that hungry I reckons as how I could eat a whole horse all by myself.

Anne : Horse! Why you old fraud! You be a proper donkey.

Tim : Does call I a donkey?

Anne (*running away left*) : Aye, that I do—a regular jackass.

Tim (*to* MR. MARTEN) : I say, Mr. Marten, is there anything allowed to eat?

Marten (*rising and throwing wide his arms in general welcome*) : Come in, young people, come in and enjoy yourselves with jolly old English cheer—roast beef and pudding and plenty of beer.

3

Tim : Ecod, I'll punish the pudding and beer.

Anne : Aye, thee great fool, thee'd punish anything.

They continue to quarrel as they go in through the cottage door followed by MEG *and* MR. AND MRS. MARTEN. MARIA *and* JOHNNY *remain outside.*

Johnny (*to left of maypole and checking—to Maria*): Are you coming in with the others, Maria?

Maria : Not just yet. I'll just sit here for a while. You go on in.

Johnny : Very well—but don't be too long. (*Goes into cottage*).

Music Cue 3—(Maria Theme softly until Cue 4).

Maria (*sitting on tree bench*): I know not what I should do. Johnny Badger loves me truly—of that I am certain although he be too shy to declare his love, but I cannot find it in my heart to love him. My dear mother chides me often and tells me that I have ideas above my station, but I have, many times, dreamed that I shall meet a handsome, wealthy gentleman and shall marry him and live happily for the rest of my days. *Music Cue 4—(Gypsy Theme).* But who is this approaching? By her dress, she would appear to be a gypsy woman.

NELL HATFIELD *enters down left. She is a middle-aged gypsy. She crosses to* MARIA *but checks downstage of maypole.*

Nell (*smiling*): Good evening to you, fair maid.

Maria : Good evening.

Nell : I am dying of thirst. May I beg a little water? I have walked twenty miles, in the hot sun, and I am very tired.

End Music Cue 4.

Maria (*rising from the bench and moving to* NELL. *She leads her to bench right.* NELL *sits*): Sit down here on the bench and I will fetch you some water (*Runs into cottage*).

Nell (*rising and moving D.R.C.*): At last—in the village where my little sister spent her happiest and darkest hours. It was here we pitched our tents. Joy and content dwelt with us and our little Zella was the sunshine of our hearts. (*Moves D.L.C.*). It was here the betrayer saw her and won her from us only to cast her off to die, heartbroken and neglected. She returned to us, but how changed was our beautiful flower. She died in my arms and with her dying breath revealed the secret of her seducer's name. (*Moving across right*). Pharos, my brother, swore vengeance on the villain who had ruined our dear sister. He swore an oath never to rest until his knife was buried in Corder's heart. The rash attempt he made to carry out his threat brought

4

the officers of the law upon us and he was forced to fly to a far off land and our tribe was dispersed and scattered. (*Returning to seat and sitting*). But my plan for revenge, being far more subtle than that of my poor brother, is the more likely to suceed.

Maria (*returning with mug of water*): Come, drink this and you will feel better (*Sits left of* NELL).

Nell : May heaven bless you, my dear. (*Drinks*). Pray tell me, fair maid, were you born here in Polstead?

Maria : That I was—here in this very cottage and have lived here all my life.

Nell : I wonder at that for you neither look nor speak like one bred in the country. There's many a gentleman, who holds his head high enough, that would be only too glad to throw himself at your feet.

Maria (*aside*): Is it possible that my dreams do not deceive me? (*Aloud*). You flatter! I am but a simple, country girl. No gentleman would think of me.

Nell : Ah, but you are mistaken; I can see in you more than you can see in yourself.

Maria : How can you tell all this?

Nell : I can see into the future and, if you will, I can teach you your destiny. By your face I already know much, but I must see your hand as well (*Takes* MARIA'S *hand and examines it*). What a delicate hand! This was never meant to be given to a peasant. Ah, I thought so—here are the lines of a fortunate marriage; riches, felicity, children are all shown here. Now let me examine your line of life. (*Looks closely*). Ah, what have we here?

Maria : What do you see?

Nell : I see signs of woe and, in the end, I see death.

Maria : Death comes to us all but woe is only caused by those who bring wretchedness upon themselves.

Nell : Fear not—your life is long enough. (*Aside*). And short enough for my purpose, I dare swear.

Maria : But can you not tell me the name of my future lover?

Nell : He is young, handsome and rich.

Maria : When shall I meet him?

Nell : You will meet him at the fair to be held here next week.

Maria : How shall I know him?

Nell : He will be wearing a white hat and carrying a cane with a dragon's head of purest silver. He will take a proper opportunity of speaking to you. Mark my words well for your whole future depends on it. (*Rises and moves D.L.C.*). But now I am rested and must be on my way. Farewell!

5

Maria: Farewell, dear kind lady. May God be with you always.

Nell : And with you. (*Turning and calling back*). Remember the fair and above all (*in a stage whisper*)—be secret! (*Checking down left*). (*Aside*). So the first part of my plan is carried out. Now to seek out the villain, Corder, and under the cloak of aiding him with his evil designs will I lead him on, step by step, until he mounts the scaffold. That will be revenge indeed! (*Exit left*).

Music Cue 5—(Intro. song).

Maria (*aside*): She has quite taken my breath away. So then, my dreams were right—I am to be a fine lady after all. Ah, could it be that, at last, I am to feel the thrill that only true love can bring?

LOVE AT LAST
(MARIA)

CHORUS

What is this strange feeling stealing through my heart,
Telling of a romance very soon to start?
I have never ever known it in the past.
Oh, could it be
That soon to me
True love will come at last?

6

I have been lonely all my life through.
Love never came before.
But if the fortune teller speaks true,
I'll be alone no more.

CHORUS

Oh, the joy of living true love can impart.
Nothing for the morrow but a carefree heart.
Will he love me ever, never let me go?
Yes, now I see
That it will be
And I will love him so.
Yes, now I see
That it will be
And I will love him so.

At end of the song MARIA *is right centre.* ANNE, MEG *and* JOHNNY *run out of the cottage laughing,* MEG *to left of* MARIA, ANNE *to left of* MEG. JOHNNY *left of maypole.*

Meg : Come along, Maria, we are going to have a bit of fun with brother Tim.

Anne : He's been telling us such stories about ghosts and goblins and murders and he says he ain't a bit frightened.

Meg : And don't I know him to be the biggest coward in all the world?

Johnny (*moving to below maypole and beckoning them to him*): Now come here all of you and listen to me (MARIA *comes to his right and* MEG *and* ANNE *to his left—they are centre stage. He whispers and they all laugh*). You, Meg and Anne—you go and hide over there. (*Indicates right*). And you Maria, you hide on that side. (*Indicates left*). I'll join you there in a minute, but first I'm off to get something that would frighten the very devil himself. (*He runs off down left*).

They take up their places as indicated by JOHNNY *behind downstage flats.*

Anne : Hush—he be coming! Now to frighten him out of his seventeen senses.

TIM *comes out of the cottage and moves to left of maypole.*

Tim (*calling back into the cottage*): Goodnight, Mr. Marten—I ain't afraid you know. Goodnight! (*Aside*). It be awful lonesome for my walk across the churchyard. I wish as how Anne had come with I and I could have held her hand. I swear I'd have brought her all the way back here as soon as I'd got home. (*Starts to move off left and checks suddenly*). No, I'm not afraid—did I not tell 'em all

7

so and I've been telling 'em all such awful stories about ghostesses and goblinesses that I've frightened 'em all into fits and, Ecod, I've frightened myself too! I'd better be going. I'll go this way.

He goes right—there is an eerie groan.

Tim : Oh, sir, that be one of them ghostesses! I ain't frightened. (*He is trembling visibly*). Go away, Mr. Ghost! (*More groans*). I'd better go t'other way. (*Moves left— groans from that side much louder*). Oh, murder! There be more ghostesses! Go away, I'm not at home! Call again tomorrow! (*Groans—louder*). Oh, murder, murder! (*On his knees*). Please, Mr. Ghost, could 'ee wait till I've said my prayers? (*Louder groans*). Them's big ghosts—it be no good me trying to go that way. (*Rises*). I'll try and see if I can get past them little ghosts on this side.

As he goes right, ANNE *and* MEG *meet him with their aprons over their heads—frightened he runs the other way.*

Tim : Oh, Lordy, Lordy me! (*Runs the other way and meets* MARIA *with her apron over her head*). Help! Help! (*Falls on ground trembling and covers his face with his hands*).

ANNE, MEG *and* MARIA *surround* TIM, *uncover their heads and roar with laughter.*

Anne: You great coward, Tim Bobbin!

Meg: Now who be frightened?

Tim (*rising*): Not I! I knew it was 'ee all the time. Now out of my way. I be off home.

As he moves left, JOHNNY *jumps out with a sheet over a pole topped with a mask and waves it in front of* TIM.

Tim: Help! Help! Help! (*Exit right pursued by others laughing*).

Music Cue 6 (Link—Maypole into Gypsy until Cue 7).

ACT ONE

SCENE TWO

A PATH IN THE WOOD NEAR THE VILLAGE—*later the same day. It is moonlight.* NELL HATFIELD *enters down left.*

Nell (*aside*): The villain comes this way. I will await his arrival here and then, if fortune favours me, will I proceed with the second part of my plan to ensnare the vile rogue who wronged my sister. He comes—now vengeance have your way ! (*Moves down left*).

Music Cue 7—(Villain Theme until Cue 8).

Enter WILLIIAM CORDER *from down stage right.*

Corder (*aside*): This way lies the cottage of the pretty maiden who has occupied my thoughts so much of late. She is coy, yet shall she be mine, for I have set my heart on possessing her.

8

THREE HISSES FOR VILLAINY
(CORDER)

I am the villain, as soon you will see.
No maiden is safe within miles of me
For I simply revel in salacity.
A double-dyed villain that's me.
All together now with me—
Three hisses for villainy.

So, if you've a daughter as fair as can be,
I'll get her although you don't let her near me
For I am an expert in lubricity.
A double-dyed villain that's me.
All together now with me—
Three hisses for villainy.

Infamy, perfidy, carnality,
Lechery, treachery, dishonesty,
All these I practise with dexterity.
A double-dyed villain that's me.
All together now with me—
Three hisses for villainy.
All together now with me—
Three hisses for villainy.

At the end of the song, CORDER *is D.S.C.).*
Nell (*moving to* CORDER *centre stage*): Good sir, a word
with you.
Corder (*aside*): What have we here, a common gypsy?
They bring no pleasant memories for me. For, once, one
of their dark-eyed beauties was partner of my journey to

9

London. Psha! She is dead; her brother attempted my life and to escape justice fled across the sea. (*Aloud*). Away, woman! I'll have no dealings with common gypsies. Be off, before I send for the officers of the law and have you, and all your filthy tribe, thrown from off the common where you have pitched your ragged tents.

Nell : For that insult I will not impart to you the knowledge that I possess of the maiden who lives in yonder cottage. (*Starts to move off left*).

Corder : Stay! Which maiden is that?

Nell (*turning*): Too late, sir. I cannot tell you now for you have seen fit to insult my tribe.

Corder : For all that, I dare swear that silver, passed across your palm, would melt the memory of that insult faster than butter in the midday sun. (*Crosses to her, takes coin from his pocket and gives it to her*). Here take this!

Nell (*spitting on the coin and putting it in her pocket*): The memory starts to fade but part of it is with me still.

Corder (*giving her another coin*): Here—but this is the last.

Nell (*aside*): Now is his interest truly aroused. I'll hesitate no longer. (*Aloud*). The maiden I speak of is called Maria Marten—she lives in the cottage hard by the village green and is the elder daughter of old Thomas Marten, the mole-catcher.

Corder (*aside*): Tis she—tis she indeed! (*Aloud*). What of her?

Nell : Earlier this evening, I told her what the fates held in store for her. She, being overjoyed at what I told her, confided in me that she secretly loved a gentleman of this parish but, being modest, dare not tell him of her love.

Corder : And what is the name of this gentleman?

Nell : Why, sir, tis none other than your good self.

Corder (*aside*): Ah, ha! Fortune seems to favour me.

Nell : She told me she would be at the fair this day week and that she prayed, most earnestly, that you might speak to her. But I near forgot—be sure that when you go to the fair you wear a white hat and carry with you a cane with a dragon's head of silver.

Corder : I will do so. And now be off with you for it grows dark and you would be well advised to reach the safety of your tent before some wandering footpad relieves you of that which you have earned today.

Nell : That which I have earned today, dear sir, is far greater than could be forfeited to any rogue that might lie in wait for me—ha! ha! ha! (*Exit left*).

Corder (*aside*): Ah, my little Maria favours me. How this unexpected turn of circumstances will ease the path for me. If Polstead Fair were tomorrow instead of this day week, it would not be soon enough for my desire. For now is my appetite whetted and I cannot wait for the day when I shall ravish her.

Music Cue 9—(Link—Villain Theme into Maypole).
Exit CORDER *right.*

ACT ONE

SCENE THREE

THE VILLAGE GREEN—*a week later, the day of Polstead Fair.*
TIM and MEG *are standing outside* MARTEN'S *cottage.*
End Music Cue 9.

Tim (*calling inside*): Anne! Maria! Be 'ee there? Meg and I has been waiting these past ten minutes or more. By the time we get to the fair 'twill be time to come home again.
Anne (*from within*): Will 'ee be patient, thou old fool. Us'll be there soon enough.
Meg (*sitting on right end of bench*): Will 'ee buy us something nice at the fair?
Tim (*sitting on her left*): That I will. I'll treat 'ee to them swing boats as goes up one side and comes down t'other, and I'll buy 'ee a pen'oth o' nuts to crack to sharpen your teeth with, and 'ee shall see all the shows — the moving waxworks and the wild beasts.
Meg: And the seven-legged calf?
Tim: Aye, and the fat woman.
Meg: Will 'ee treat us to all that?
Tim: That I will, sister Meg. I've got a power of brass. (*Aside*): I've naught but a shilling.

> MARIA *and* ANNE *come out of the cottage, dressed in their best clothes and sweep past* TIM *and* MEG *to centre stage.*

Anne: Come along, Tim Bobbin, hurry up! Be 'ee going to sit there all night?

> MEG *rises and moves to join* MARIA *and* ANNE.

Tim (*getting up from bench*): Well, jumping Jiminy, if women don't beat the lot. Here we've been waiting for 'ee half the day and now 'ee tells I to hurry up.

> MARIA, ANNE *and* MEG *move right while* TIM *is talking.*

Anne: Come along, Tim Bobbin—how slow you walk.
Tim: Tis the weight of money I've got in my pocket that keeps I back.
Maria (*moving to right of* TIM): What are you going to buy us for a fairing?
Tim: Why, Maria, I'll buy 'ee a monkey up a stick.
Anne: She don't want one, Tim, while thou be with her.
Tim: Ah, 'ee dinna say so?

11

Anne (*moving to his left and putting her head on his shoulder*): And what will 'ee buy I?

Tim : I'll buy 'ee a cradle.

Anne : A cradle? What for?

Tim : Agen us get wed.

Meg : If us be going to the fair, let's be off at once or go home.

Tim : There's a public house on the road and if 'ee be good, I'll treat 'ee all.

Meg : But I don't drink beer.

Anne: Nor I.

Maria : Nor I.

Tim : Then, as I say I'll treat 'ee.

Anne : Treat us to what, thou old fool?

Tim : Why, to the pleasure of seeing I drink it—come on! *They all move off right.*

Maria (*checking*): But a moment—I've forgotten my scarf. I'll just go and get it from the cottage. You be on your way —I'll catch you up before you've reached the turning in the lane. (*Runs into cottage*).

Meg : Come along then for I can scarce wait to see that fat woman.

Tim : Nor I to find that public house.

Anne (*dragging him off*): I'll give 'ee public house!

ANNE, TIM *and* MEG *go off right.*

Music Cue 10—(Villain Theme).

CORDER *enters left and moves to centre stage.*

Corder (*aside*): As the gypsy woman foretold, the sweet Maria is going to the fair. Hiding behind yonder tree, I overheard all that befell. I have but to wait here to accost the maiden when she emerges from her cottage and matters stand well for my wooing.

End Music Cue 10.

MARIA *comes out of the cottage and starts to run right.*

Corder (*standing in her path*): Miss Marten, I see you are on your way to the fair.

Maria : Indeed yes, sir—but I must hurry or my friends will be there before me. (*Aside*). This must be the gentleman of whom the gypsy spoke.

Corder : Perhaps you would accept my humble services as escort?

Maria: But, sir, that would never do for I know you not.

Corder: I am the son of your father's landlord—my name is William Corder. I assure you that I wish you nothing but good.

Maria: But whatever would folks say to see Maria Marten, the molecatcher's daughter, in company with the son of the rich Mr. Corder?

Corder: They would say that William Corder has too much manhood to see a poor maiden go unprotected in such a scene of wild confusion. Why, I declare, Maria, you look uncommonly pretty today. That white dress becomes you well.

Maria: Thank you, kind sir.

Corder (*aside*): Now for a plan to delay our departure and have the maiden to myself. (*Aloud*). Let us be on our way then for I—I—I (*He starts to stagger*).

Maria : What ails you, sir?

Corder : Tis nothing—just a little giddiness. The day is uncommonly hot. I'll just sit here under the shade of this tree and I'll soon recover. (*Sits on right side of tree seat*). (*Aside*): My plan succeeds most excellently. By now the other bumpkins will be at the fair and I shall have the maiden to myself. Ha! Ha!. (*Aloud*): Come, sit beside me whilst I rest for a moment.

Maria : But for a short while then, for I am most anxious to find my friends. (*Sits on his left*).

Corder : Upon my word, Maria, now that you are sitting here by my side, I declare that I feel a great deal better already (*Tries to take her hand*). Maria, I am quite in love with you.

Maria (*taking away her hand*): Nonsense—do not be so foolish!

Corder : I think I am very wise. I assure you that I love you dearly, that I want a wife and if you'll have me I'll make you as comfortable as you could ever wish.

Maria : Why, Mr. Corder, what would you do with a wife?

Corder : Leave that to me. I'll tell you when you marry me.

Maria (*rising and moving D.S.C.*): Then, I fear, I am never likely to know.

Corder (*rising and moving to her right*): If you marry me, I'll make you as happy as a queen. You know that my family is well off and we should want for nothing.

Maria (*aside*): Tis all happening as the gypsy said. But I must not appear too anxious for fear that Mr. Corder think me a forward girl. (*Aloud*). Let us say no more of this for the present. I must find my sister Anne and Tim and his sister Meg. You promised me that you would assist me in my search for them.

Corder : Most certainly I will. As we pass along, I'll tell you the difference between these rural sports and the gay sights of London—the balls, the concerts, the theatres and all the joys that make life worth living.

Maria : How I should love to live in London.

LONDON TOWN
(MARIA)

Is it true what I've been told—
All the streets are paved with gold?
Is it right that in that town,
London Bridge is falling down?
London Town, London Town,
That is the place I'd love to see.
London Town, London Town,
That's where I long to be.

I would dearly love to go
Where they ride in Rotten Row,
See the palace of the King,
Listen to the Bow Bells ring.
London Town, London Town,
That is the place I'd love to see.
London Town, London Town,
That's where I long to be.

But I doubt if it can be
That a country girl like me
Ever will to London go.
Simple life is all I'll know.
London Town, London Town,
That is the place I'd love to see.
London Town, London Town,
That's where I long to be.

14

Corder : Who knows, one day, you may live there. If you would consent to marry me—

Maria : I thought that we had agreed to speak no more of that for the time being.

Corder : As you wish, my little Maria, but at least promise me that, after the fair, you will permit me the pleasure of seeing you home. Who knows what might become of you on the road. The fair will be crowded with drunken labourers and gypsy vagrants. Nay—no refusal! I'll see you safely home to your own door.

Maria : Come along then (*Runs off right*).

Corder (*aside*): And so is my first step gained. (*Exit right*). *Music Cue 12 — (Villain Theme loudly into Gypsy Theme*).

Thunder and lightning. NELL HATFIELD *appears down left.*

Nell : Aye—your first step towards the ladder of crime you are about to mount. When you have reached the summit, then will my cup of vengeance be filled. Ha! Ha! Ha!

Music Cue 13—(Link—Gypsy Theme into I Ain't As Daft).

ACT ONE

SCENE FOUR

A CLEARING IN THE WOOD—*twelve months later. It is dusk and owl calls are heard.* TIM *enters left. He is tipsy and staggers across to stage right where there is a tree stump. End Music Cue 13.*

Tim : I wonder where my sweetheart be. Her promised to meet I by the blackberry bush, but her dinna come. I shouldn't wonder if her ain't gone out with another chap, and left I to die an old maid. I've been down to the 'Cat and Fiddle' and had some ale and then I met the parish beadle and he threatened to put I in the stocks for being drunk and disorderly, so I comes down the lane, and here I stays till my Anne comes. (*Sits on tree stump, falls off and after a few more unsuccessful attempts, sits on ground and leans against the stump*).

Enter MEG *from left and moves to centre stage.*

Meg (*aside*): Well, I'm blest if I ain't lost my way. My ma sent I down to these parts to see if I could find that foolish brother of mine who her afeared had got himself lost in the woods and, bless me, if it ain't got dark and I can't find my way out again.

Tim (*singing in a slurred voice*): Meet me by moonlight alone—al-oo-ne!

15

Meg (*backing away left*): Why, I do believe it be Tim.
(*Aloud*). Tim, be that 'ee? Where be 'ee?

Tim : Over here, by this old tree stump.

Meg (*crossing to him*): Whatever be 'ee doing there?

Tim : I be waiting for my sweetheart, but I reckon as
how her ain't be coming. I'd best be on my way home (*Trys
to stand and falls down again*).

Meg (*pulling him up and supporting him*): Now, brother
Tim, has 'ee been drinking again?

Tim : Well, I did happen to call in at the 'Cat and Fiddle'
but I only had one or two.

Meg : One or two gallons I'd say by the looks of 'ee.
Come on, I'll steady 'ee as we go home.

Tim : Aye 'ee lead the way, for the road home has gone
clean out of my head.

Meg : Tim Bobbin, do 'ee mean to stand there and tell I
as 'ee don't know the way home?

Tim : No—and that's for sure.

Meg : Then what be us going to do, for I be lost myself?
Us can't stay here all night. I be mortal scared of these
woods after sunset.

Tim : Ah, this be a right problem and no mistake.
(*Scratching his head*). What can us do? Now let I think a
minute—ah, I have it!

Meg : What, Tim?

Tim : We'll off home and ask Ma. Her's bound to know
the way for her be older than we.

Meg : Now that's a grand idea, brother Tim—come on
then. (*Leads him to right and exits*).

Tim (*following her and then checking and addressing
audience with a wink*). You see I ain't as daft as some folks
say.

    Music Cue 14—(Song).

I AIN'T AS DAFT AS SOME FOLKS SAY
(TIM BOBBIN)

I ain't as daft as some folks say.
I'm sort of clever in my simple way.

I went for a new job, one fine sunny morn.
The farmer said 'Tim, lad, now you sow the corn,'
'Do you think I be daft' to the farmer, I said.
'How can I sow the corn when I ain't got no thread?'
I ain't as daft as some folks say.
I'm sort of clever in my simple way.

'Go out to the pigs now,' said old Farmer Bill.
'Take out that there bucket and give 'em their swill.'
But I swilled and I swilled till I can't swill no more
And I reckons they'm dirtier than they was afore.
I ain't as daft as some folks say.
I'm sort of clever in my simple way.

One morning, the farmer's wife to I she said,
'Go dig up some taters from out of the bed.'
So I digged and I digged until I was quite hot,
But two big piles of feathers was all that I got.
I ain't as daft as some folks say.
I'm sort of clever in my simple way.

One day the old farmer to I he did say,
'Now, Tim boy, I wants 'ee to get in the hay.'
So, I tells the old farmer I'se pleased to obey
And I takes off my boots and I lies there all day.
I ain't as daft as some folks say.
I'm sort of simple in my clever way.

Music Cue 15—(Gypsy Theme until Cue 16).

NELL HATFIELD *enters down left.*

Nell (*aside*): So far my plan has succeeded beyond my wildest dreams. Maria Marten has fallen victim of Corder, and a child—the offspring of her shame—has been born. But Corder already wearies of his plaything. Last night, he came to our tents to purchase a deadly poison known only to those of our tribe. I hear that the child is ill and I believe that I know what his plan of action will be. I promised to procure the poison and arranged to meet him here. Oh, I'll watch him like a lynx, for the stars tell me that the hour of retribution is at hand.
Music Cue 16—(Villain Theme).

17

Enter CORDER *right.*

Corder (*aside*): She is here. Now will I proceed to business. (*Aloud—crossing to* NELL *who meets him centre stage*). Have you the drug of which we spoke yesterday?

Nell : The poison—yes.

Corder : And can you answer, truthfully, for its effect?

Nell: That I can. I have seen it used on both man and beast alike.

End Music Cue 16.

Corder : And know you for what purpose I require this drug?

Nell (*aside*): That I do, only too well.

Corder : I have a dog which I fear I must destroy for it has been worrying the farmers' sheep.

Nell : One drop of this is sufficient to kill twenty men. and its effect is as swift and sudden as the lightning. What is more, it leaves no trace behind of its deadly work and oft has defied the skill of the most learned doctors.

Corder : Tis well. Here is the gold I promised. (*Gives her a purse and* NELL *gives him the poison bottle*). Now go! Let our paths, from now, be divided and forget that you have ever seen my face. Henceforth, we are strangers— never forget that!

Nell : So be it. Farewell kind, generous gentleman, fare- well. (*Aside*). Now will I watch his every action. Nothing will I fail to see. I'll watch and watch and watch! (*Exit left*).

Music Cue 17—(Villain Theme Loudly).

Corder : (*aside*): This poison must I use this very night. Maria has written to me with news that the child is ill. For the sake of our mutual safety—it must die. *End Music Cue 17.* As yet, the people of the village know not the child is Maria's. They think it to be a child she has taken in to nurse. Should all be known, my father, with his strict ideas of honour and virtue, would drive me from the house and cut me from his will. The child must die and Maria shall be my accomplice. I will bury it in the woods, for an inquest might reveal to the world that which I would not have known. What if Maria should have scruples—what of that? Then the child will be my first victim and the mother fall the second. (*Exit right*).

Nell (*entering left*): Tis as I suspected. He takes the path towards the house where he has lodged Maria Marten to hide her shame. Now is my revenge about to triumph. Look down, spirit of my broken-hearted Zella, from thy home among the stars and steel thy sister's heart to make thy betrayer's scaffold thy monument!

Music Cue 18—(Link Gypsy Theme into Maria Theme).

18

ACT ONE

SCENE FIVE

INTERIOR OF A COTTAGE—*later the same day. There is a table upstage centre with one chair above it and another to the left. There is a cradle downstage right to the left of which* MARIA *is kneeling.*

Music Cue 18 continues until song.

Maria : Another day passes and he comes not. Oh my child, my child, would that thy heartbroken mother and thyself could sink to sleep and peace for ever! But twelve short months ago, I was a happy village girl. What am I today? (*Rising*). I am a betrayed, ruined woman scorned by all who know my shame.

Music Cue 19—(Song).

DESERTED AND LONELY
(MARIA)

Deserted and lonely,
Here in my shame,
Will you not come back to me
And give my child a name?
Oh, how I miss you,
Words can never say.
But, to you, I'll e'er be true
Through every lonely day.

So this is my prayer then.
Oh, heed it do.

Let me see thy face again
Before my life is through.
Thy child is waiting,
Little arms outstretched,
Waiting for you to return
To clasp him to thy breast.
Waiting for you to return
To clasp him to thy breast.

Oh my poor, poor father, what disgrace have I not brought on thee? (*Moving to below chair left*). But William shall marry me—I hold his promise. (*Sinks into chair*). He shall give me back my honour or—or—(*Bursts into tears*).
There is a knock on the door left.
Ah, someone is at the door—perhaps tis he. (*Rises*).
Enter ANNE *and* TIM *left.*
Anne (*crossing to left of* MARIA): Hello, Maria, it's I.
Tim: And it's I, too.
Maria (*embracing her*): Yes and Tim, thy brother-in-law that is to be.
Anne: Shut up, thou big fool! (*To* MARIA) I was going by and called in to see thee.
Maria: And most welcome you are, dearest Anne and Tim. Come sit down. (ANNE *sits above table and* MARIA *left*).
Tim (*moving down to cradle*): I'm going to have a look at the baby.
Anne: Get off with thee—what's thee want with a baby?
Tim: Why, to get my hand in, to be sure.
Maria (*rising*): Nan, I hope you have kept my secret. So far everyone believes this to be a child I have taken in to nurse. You have told no one different?
Anne: No, I have told no one—that is except for Tim.
Tim: And I have told no one—that is except for my brother Bob and my sister Meg and they have told no one —that is except for my sixteen cousins and they told no one—that is except for—
Anne: Oh, thou great fool! But, Maria, I really came to tell thee that Mother and Father said that they would be coming here this very evening.
Maria (*moving down left*): No, no, they must not come here! (*Facing away from* ANNE). They must not see me in my shame. My mother's grey hair will seem to speak reproaches and tell of her virtuous life, now disgraced by my misdeed. And, Father! I swear that I should die beneath his stern gaze.
Anne (*rising and moving down to right of* MARIA): Come, cheer up, Maria. It won't be as bad as you think. I have broken the news to our parents.

20

Maria : What said they?

Anne : Father lifted up his eyes to Heaven and said 'Oh, merciful God, my poor girl then is ruined.'

Maria : And Mother—what said she?

Anne : She cried a great deal at first but then she said that you were still her child, though fallen in sin through a villain's means.

Tim (*calling*): Anne! Maria! Come here, at once, and look at the baby.

MARIA *and* ANNE *run across right.*

Maria (*kneeling right of cradle*): What is it? My poor child has been ailing of late. What is the matter?

Tim : It's just opened its mouth!

Maria : Yes?

Tim : And it ain't got no teeth.

Anne : Get along with you, thou old fool, Little 'uns like that don't have no teeth.

Tim : Then how does they eats their bread and butter? Oh, look, look! !

Maria : What ails it now?

Tim : It's head is as bald as a duck egg. Look now—it's opening its mouth again. Give it the knob of the kitchen poker to suck.

Anne : Tim Bobbin, would 'ee have the baby as big a fool as thee? Thy mother used to give thee the knob of the wooden bedstead to suck and thee'st been wooden-headed ever since (*Taps him on his head with her knuckles*).

Knock at door left.

Maria (*rising*): Who can that be?

Anne : I expect it be the old folks. Us'll be away then. Come along, Tim.

Tim : I want to stop and nurse the baby.

Anne : Nonsense, you'll drop it and give it the gravel rash. Can us go out the back way, Maria? I don't want Mother and Father to know us has been here afore them.

Maria : Of course—this is the way. (*Moving up right followed by* ANNE).

Anne : And you, Tim, leave the baby be and come along afore you frighten the poor little mite out of its senses.

Tim (*as he moves up to* ANNE): I never saw such a funny thing of a little baby afore. It's got no teeth and it's bald-headed. But it's just like William Corder—I can tell by its nose.

Anne (*pulling* TIM *off right*): Come along, thou old fool!

Exit TIM *and* ANNE *up right. Another knock at the door.*

MARIA *moves to above cradle.*

Maria (*aside*): Oh how I dread the meeting. But heart be firm—they come!

21

Music Cue 20—(*Maria Theme slowly*). *Enter* MRS.
MARTEN *and* MARTEN *left.*

Maria (*moving to centre stage and falling on her knees*):
Once more, do I see the faces of those most dear to me.
(*With arms outstretched*). Father, Mother—your unhappy
child implores your forgiveness.

Mrs. Marten (*moving to left of* MARIA *and raising her gently
to her feet*): Unhappy girl, a mother's heart is more indul-
gent than the world's but there is one yet to be appeased—
your father.

Marten (*moving down left centre*): Oh, how I doted on
thee, daughter, there are no words to express, but you
sacrificed me for a villain. Your ingratitude has bleached
my head and broken my heart.

Maria (*moving to* MARTEN): Dear Father—no more. In
mercy I beseech you—no more!
End Music Cue 20.

Marten : As I gaze on thee, I think of thy infant days
when your first little steps began. When laughingly, with
outstretched arms, you ran towards me and I trembled lest
your feet should fail. You escaped those and a thousand
other dangers but now you fall—fall to earth never to rise
again.

Mrs. M. (*to right of Maria and putting her arm around
her*): But our child is repentant. I beg you to speak a word
of comfort to her.

Marten (*turning down left*): Did I not train her in the path
of virtue? Did I not press her to this doting heart and in
my foolish pride proclaim my child to be a paragon of all
the virtues? (*Turning to* MARIA). And did she not blast all
my fond hopes and, clinging to a villain, leave me in my
storm of grief? Oh, I feel that I could curse the day—

Maria : No! No! Your vengeance cannot make you deaf
to the agony of a despairing child! (*On knees*). Behold me
once more, on my knees, begging you to have mercy and
charity in your heart for your own flesh and blood, even
though her young feet have strayed from the straight path
you taught her to walk. I do not ask your love until you
know that I am worthy of it, but do not, dear father of
mine, deny me the shelter of your paternal roof.

Mrs. M. : Dear husband, do not aggravate the girl's
misery. You must see that she is repentant. She is the shorn
lamb. Do not add another wound to her poor heart that is
so severely lacerated.

Maria : Bless you, Mother, bless you for those words.

Marten : Very well. Maria, I forgive thee. We are all
sinners and should be merciful in our judgment of each
other.

22

Maria (*rising*): Father—dear Father!

Marten : Thy father's arms, thy father's home are both open to receive thee.

They fall into each others arms D.L.C.

Mrs. M. : Come, child, return to your home at once.

Maria : I cannot!

Mrs. M. : Why not, my child? You have received your father's forgiveness. You are once more welcome in the home of your childhood.

Maria : I await the arrival of my William.

Marten (*moving down left*): Believe not in that villain who has thus deceived and betrayed thee.

Maria : Nay, that is not true. A thousand times has he sworn to marry me. It is only for family reasons that our union has been delayed. He may be here at any moment.

Mrs. M. (*crossing to* MARTEN): Come, husband, we will leave her now. Let us hope for the best and be patient.

Marten : Hope? I am the scathed tree of the heath that cannot drop. The bolt that struck off my branches has left my trunk erect in wretched loneliness. Come, wife!

They exit left. MARIA *moves to centre stage.*

Maria (*aside*): The forgiveness of my father has lightened my heart. Oh, that my William would fulfil his promise— then happiness would indeed be mine. (*Crossing to cradle*). And how is my dear child? Of late, I fear that thou hast been ailing. I am most worried and have sent a message to your father begging him to come. (*Footsteps off left*). Ah, 'tis he!

Music Cue 21—(Villain Theme).

Enter CORDER *left.*

Corder (*crossing to* MARIA *by cradle*): Dear Maria, I received your note and hastened to you. How is the child?

Maria : Ill—very ill. I fear it may not be long for this world. If you do not make me an honest woman, I wish no more of life.

End Music Cue 21.

Corder : Have I not sworn to thee, by every sacred vow, that thou shalt be my wife? My father hovers o'er the grave. He dead, I'll make you mine at once and our child shall be a bond to our union.

Maria : I believe you, dear William.

Corder : I swear it. (*They embrace*).

Maria : But, William, dearest, why have you not brought the doctor as I requested?

Corder (*moving away to centre stage*) (*aside*): Now must I act with great caution if I am to allay suspicion. (*Aloud*). He could not attend today. He will call tomorrow. I

23

showed him your note and he wrote out a prescription for a medicine that, he said, would remove all pain for the present. I went to the apothecary in the village and he prepared it for me. I have it here. (*Produces bottle from his pocket*).

Maria (*going to* CORDER *and taking bottle*): My dear William, this is most kind of you. I will administer it at once.

Corder : Do so, Maria. (*Moves down left*).

MARIA *fetches a spoon from the table and gives a dose from the bottle to the baby.*

Corder (*aside*): Now shall we see if the gypsy woman spoke the truth. If so, then will my troubles be at an end.

Maria : The little one seems soothed already. See how peacefully it sleeps.

CORDER *crosses to left of* MARIA.

Corder (*aside*): The potion works indeed.

Maria : William, my mother and father have been here today. They are heartbroken at my shame.

Corder : Fear not, girl, all will be well.

Maria (*kneeling down by cradle*): What ails the child—tis convulsed?

Corder : Do not distress yourself so.

Maria : But 'tis ill! It does not move! (*Screams*). 'Tis. dead! (*Falls across cradle*). My little one is dead!

Corder : You must be mistaken. It but sleeps.

Maria (*rising*): No—the child is dead—my little one is no more. (*Looks at bottle which she still holds in her hand*). What is this—'tis marked 'poison?' This bottle in which you brought the medicine from the apothecary is marked 'poison!'

Corder : Marked 'poison?' (*Aside*). Why would that fool of a gypsy woman have labelled the bottle thus? (*Aloud*). I know nothing of this.

Maria (*showing* CORDER *the bottle*): Look here—'poison!' Do you not see?

Corder (*striking his head with his hands*): Great God, what have I done? Oh, Maria, it was a dreadful mistake. I purchased the medicine for the infant and, at the same time, brought some poison for rats.

Maria : Poison for rats?

Corder : Do you not see? It was the rat poison I gave to you by mistake. The other I must have left at home. (*Aside*). By this artifice, will I attempt to conceal the truth. (*Moves away left*).

Maria : Oh, Heaven save us—what is to be done?

Corder: I must think—I must think! Ah, I believe I may

have the solution to our dreadful dilemma. The manner of the poor child's death is known to no other than ourselves —thus it must remain. We must keep it a secret from the world.

Maria : But how?

Corder : We must tell the old people that the infant died of a convulsion so suddenly that timely aid could not be obtained. The child must be buried with all convenient speed. We must bury it secretly where none will find it.

Maria : Oh, William, I could not do such a deed.

Corder : We must — we have no other choice, for the manner of its death might be betrayed by some palpable marks on its body.

Maria : But, William—my poor child—will it not lie in hallowed ground?

Corder : We must waste no more time. I will hasten to make the necessary preparations and we must proceed, this very night, to a secret part of the wood to lay the child in its last resting place. (*Aside*). The child is dead and I am safe!

Music Cue 22—(Gypsy Theme).

NELL HATFIELD *appears left.*

Nell (*aside*): No, William Corder — not safe but lost eternally in the eyes of Heaven. Another fatal step on the ladder of crime!

MARIA *sinks over the cradle weeping.*

Music Cue 23—(Link—Deserted and Lonely into Villain Theme slowly).

ACT ONE

SCENE SIX

THE WOOD—*late evening of the same day. It is moonlight and the sound of an owl screeching is heard from time to time throughout this scene. There is a small hillock upstage centre.* CORDER *enters right carrying a spade. He is followed by* MARIA *who is clasping a small bundle.*

Corder (*crossing to above hillock*): This place will serve our purpose well. Here, behind this hillock, will we dig the grave. (*He begins to dig*).

End Music Cue 23.

Maria : William, this is a dreadful deed!

Corder: But, for the safety of us both, it must be done.

Maria (*standing right of* CORDER): My poor infant, to leave it here in this lonely place is terrible.

Corder : Believe me, 'tis for the best. An inquest might tell more than we should like the world to know and a magistrate's enquiry would harm you more than I. There is a severe penalty for the concealment of a birth.

25

Maria : Am I not in your power? But it is hard for my little one to be here.

Corder ; Nonsense! The child will sleep as peacefully here as in the graveyard. (*Stops digging and straightens up*). Ah, the grave is large enough now.

Voice (*from off left—sepulchral*): Too large—too large by far!

MARIA *sinks to the ground*, CORDER *drops the spade and goes left to look off.*

Corder (*calling*): Who are you? Answer, I charge you! Who are you? (*After a pause*). There is no reply. (*Returns to behind hillock*). Quick, we must complete the deed and away from here with all dispatch.

He takes the bundle from MARIA *puts it into the grave and covers it over.*

Corder : 'Tis done! (MARIA *picks up a stick and pushes it in the ground behind the hillock*). Why do you push that stick into the ground?

Maria : I am marking the spot so that later I may return and strew the little grave with flowers.

Corder : That would be most unwise. Hurry, we are not safe here!

Music Cue 24—(Maria Theme softly).

Maria (*kneeling*): Farewell, farewell, my dearest child. May the angels up above guard thee. Never, never shall I see thee more.

End Music Cue 24.

Corder :' (*moving right*): Maria—come at once!

Maria (*rising and moving across to* CORDER): I come. William, I have great fear. What could that voice have been?

Corder : 'Twas nothing but the echo of this lonely place.

Maria : No—that could not be. I believe it to have been the voice of a spirit.

Corder : Nonsense. Come, we must away. (*They move to exit right*).

Maria (*checking and looking back*): I am sore afraid.

Corder (*ushering her off right*): Stupid girl—there is no eye that beholds us now. Come! (*They go off right*).

Music Cue 25—(Gypsy Theme).

Enter NELL HATFIELD *from down left.*

(*At this point, if traverse curtains are used, they can be opened to enable the full stage to be used for the gypsy scene which follows. Cut-out trees could be set during the first half of this scene*).

Nell (*aside*): There you are mistaken, William Corder. There is one eye that sees your every deed. 'Tis the eye of

26

Nell Hatfield, the gypsy—and vengeance will be mine. Did you not rob me of my sister, Zella, and send my brother a wanderer across the sea? For these deeds, will I make you an outcast, strip you of your fortune and let you suffer the pangs of despised beggary we suffer. (*To centre stage*). I'll drag you to the scaffold foot, then, with my vengeful eyes glaring into yours and my cry of bitter mockery ringing in your ears, I'll force you to mount, step by step, until I place the rope around your neck. Then shall I watch you die and pray that your death will be a long, torturous one.

End Music Cue 25.

PETRA, CARMEN *and* ROSA, *three gypsy women, rush in from the right.*

Petra (*running to* NELL): Nell! Nell! We bring you fearful tidings.

Rosa: We have been driven from the common by the officers of the law, acting for this William Corder.

Nell: Driven from the common?

Carmen: Aye, 'tis true. But, ere we go, our men have sworn vengeance, full and deep.

Rosa: Aye, vengeance! Vengeance!

Petra: Our men will strike the blow surely. This Corder heeded not our cries nor those of our children—why then should we spare his life? This very night shall Corder's eyes be closed in the sleep of death.

Gypsies: Vengeance! Vengeance! (*They start to run off left*).

Nell: Hold! Whither you go?

Rosa: To join our menfolk. This William Corder has set the police upon us, hunted us like wild beasts from the land his good father allowed us to pitch our tents upon. And for resistance, many of our men lie in the jail. So Corder's life must answer for it.

Nell (*crossing to them*): Hold! Hold I say—this must not be!

Carmen: What mean you?

Nell: That particular revenge is mine! I claim it for my own!

Rosa: Our husbands cry for vengeance within their prison cells. Shall they cry in vain?

Nell: Not so. He has stacks of wheat and hay. Give them and all the barns and his house to the flames. Make him a beggar and that complete, I will reveal a secret that will put the hangman's noose around his neck.

Carmen: Tell us the nature of the secret.

Nell: Nay—I will not tell you my secret yet—not until the work of desolation is complete. Go now—tell our brothers

to set fire to all that this Corder owns in life and then, when
that is done, return here and I will give you proof that will
drag Corder to a murderer's doom.

Rosa : We will—'tis a glorious plan. We go to tell the men
to fetch blazing torches and carry them to Corder's farm.

Petra : Before we strike our tents tonight, the lights to
guide us on the road shall be the blazing embers of the
villain's home.

PETRA, CARMEN *and* ROSA *exit left.*

Nell (*aside*): After all these years of watching and waiting,
nemesis has come at last.

Music Cue 26—(Villain Theme).

CORDER *steps out from stage right where he has been
hiding.*

Corder (*aside*): The traitor! 'Tis fortunate that I overheard
all that was said. Could it be that she watched me when I
buried the child? If that be so, she is the only witness for
Maria dare not speak. (*Aloud—advancing on* NELL *who is
centre stage*). So, hag, you would betray me eh?

End Music Cue 26.

Nell : Corder! Aye, I would betray you and drive you a
beggar from your home!

Corder (*laughing*): That threat can only give me cause for
laughter. The farm and all its contents are insured to full
value, so they can go to the devil, as far as I am concerned.

Nell : You laugh too soon. You forget that your life is
still in my power.

Corder (*laughing*): My life?

Nell : Yes, I am the sister of that poor girl whom you so
basely betrayed. I am the sister of the lad you drove to
exile.

Corder : You lie!

Nell : Not I! I swore that I would have my revenge—
it is now at hand. I dogged you, step by step. I saw you
poison Maria Marten's child and, this very night, observed
you as you buried it here in this wood. All that now
remains is for me to bring the officers here and your life
is forfeit.

Corder : So is yours, traitor! (*Produces a pistol and shoots*
NELL *who falls to the ground. He moves to right—aside*).
So perish the only witness to my crime and I can walk the
world without a fear of betrayal from any lips. This has
been a good night's work indeed. (*Exit right*).

PETRA, CARMEN *and* ROSA *run on from left—*ROSA *crosses
to up right.*

Rosa : What was that shot? It seemed to come from some-
where hereabouts. (*Turns and sees* NELL *lying on the
ground*). Ah, 'tis Nell—see she bleeds!

28

They kneel on each side of her and support her.
Petra : Who has done this—tell us who has done this?
Nell (*fighting for breath*): 'Twas—'twas—
Carmen : Yes, yes—tell us!
Nell : I am dying—but while I still have life will I say his name—William Corder!
Petra : Corder!
Nell : Promise me—promise me—
Rosa : Anything—but name it.
Nell (*haltingly*): Swear to seek out my brother, Pharos, who was banished overseas. Swear, by the mystic powers of our tribe, to find him and tell him to relentlessly pursue the path of vengeance until mine and my sister's deaths are revenged. Swear!
Gypsies : We swear!
Nell : 'Tis well—'tis well. My eyes grow dim. My blood is chilled and the spirit of my dear departed sister, Zella, calls me to her home among the stars.
Carmen : But this secret you know of William Corder—reveal it to us ere you die.
Nell (*gasping*): Corder—Corder—he is a—a—a— (*falls back*).
Rosa : The spirit has broken from its earthly prison—the doors of death are open wide. She has gone to join our brothers and sisters of the great tribe above.
Music Cue 27—(Song).

A GYPSY LAMENT

(PETRA, CARMEN AND ROSA)

Oh, the spirit now has fled
And our sister lies here dead.
No more sorrow, no more pain
Will she ever know again.

Branded for all time you be,
When you're born a Romany.
But her wandering days are o'er.
She has entered Heaven's door.

Let the moon up in the sky
Hide its face before we cry.
For the dirge must now be sung
And the funeral bell be rung.

Petra (*rising and looking out left*): Ah, see the farm burns!
*There is a red glow from offstage left. The stage lights
fade.*
Rosa : The moon has veiled her face. Let us lift up our eyes
and look steadily to the west!
Repeat last verse of song.

CURTAIN

Music Cue 28—(Entr'acte).

ACT TWO

SCENE ONE

Music Cue 29—(Maria Theme softly).
THE MARTENS' KITCHEN—*a week later. There is an armchair set right and another left. There is a small table centre stage.* MARIA *is seated right.*
This scene is set below the traverse.

Maria: I wonder if William will call today. I have an appalling premonition of some impending tragedy. My nights are sleepless and I think constantly of my poor child in Heaven. *End Music Cue 29.* (*Rising and moving centre stage*). How strange it is that the village apothecray should have no knowledge of the medicine that William told me he obtained from him on that fateful day. I cannot rid myself of the horrid image that William could have intended to poison my poor, poor child. (*Moving left*). But—no!—no!—that is impossible! There must be some explanation that is so simple that I fail to recognise it. I will mention the matter to him when he calls. (*Turning*). Ah—a footstep I know—'tis he!

Music Cue 30—(Villain Theme).
CORDER *enters down right carrying a carpet bag.*

Corder (*aside*):- Curse the girl, she has been making enquiries of the apothecary. Who knows but that she might aquaint others of what she has learnt. I fear that there is no safety for me while she lives. *End Music Cue 30.* (*Aloud*). Well, my little Maria, I have come for you at last We must go—so get ready at once. (*To centre stage*).

Maria (*moving centre and embracing him*): Oh, William, you have kept the promise so long made to me.

Corder: The death of my father has removed the only obstacle to our union.

Maria (*moving away left*): I'll aquaint my parents with the joyful tidings.

Corder (*crossing to her and catching hold of her arm*): One moment, Maria, you know the aversion my mother has to your family. Therefore, to keep our marriage a secret from her, I wish the ceremony to be performed in London.

Maria : London? Why there?

Corder : Business of great importance calls me away this very night—you must be my companion. (*Opening bag and removing costume*). I wish you to put on this suit of male attire and meet me tonight at the old Red Barn.

31

Music Cue 31—(Villain Theme slowly).
Maria : The old Red Barn! No, no, not there I beg of you! Even as a child when I played about it, its shadow cast a chill upon me.
End Music Cue 31.
Corder : Never fear—from the Red Barn we start on our road to love and happiness.
Maria : But to leave in the dark and in male attire! Why this mystery, dear William?
Corder : For the purpose of avoiding observation. You will put on this attire and then proceed to the Red Barn. I will follow when I have fetched a few of my belongings from the farm.
Maria : Very well, I consent. But, William, you will not be long in joining me?
Corder : No, dearest. (*Aside*). Little does she know what plans I have for her at the Red Barn. (*Aloud*). At the Red Barn, you will resume your female dress which you will carry thither in this bag.
Maria : As you wish, dear William. (*Takes the bag and the clothes*). I'll go upstairs, change my dress and send my parents down to you.
Corder : Hurry then for there is no time to be lost.
Exit MARIA *left.*
Corder (*moving down right—aside*): She consents—one point gained. Curse the girl, she enquires too much and binds me down.

Music Cue 32—(Song)

CURSE THE GIRL
(CORDER)

Curse, the girl, curse the girl,
She starts to bind me down.
Curse the girl, curse the girl,
I must get out of town.

Curse the girl, curse the girl,
My fortune I have lost.
Curse the girl, curse the girl,
I cannot bear the cost.

Curse the girl, curse the girl,
Curses on her head.
Curse the girl, curse the girl,
A rich wife I must wed.

Curse the girl, curse the girl,
I curse her every day.
Curse the girl, curse the girl,
She's getting in my way.

Curse the girl, curse the girl,
She's started now to pry.
Curse the girl, curse the girl,
I fear she'll have to die!

Spoken: CURSE THE GIRL!

Corder : Maria Marten, when you consented to meet me in the Red Barn, you settled your doom. (*He moves to the table, takes a pistol from his pocket and starts to examine it*).
Enter MARTEN *left—moves to left of* CORDER.
Marten : Ah, William, is this true? Maria tells me that you are about to keep your promise.
Corder (*moving to hide the pistol behind his back*): 'Tis true, Mr. Marten.
Marten : 'Tis a generous, noble act. William, I thank thee; give me thy hand. (*Takes* CORDER'S *hand and holds it*). The poor old father's tears will cease to flow when gazing on his children and his household happy all around him. To you I'll owe it all. I give thee, then, a father's blessing.
Corder : Thank thee, thank thee, Father.
Marten: But what is that you have there—a pistol?
Corder (*putting it in his pocket*): Why yes, I never travel without it. (*Aside*). Little does he know how soon I shall have need of it. (*Moves to right centre*).
Enter MRS. MARTEN *left*.
Mrs. M. : I am glad to hear the news, William. The poor girl has too long borne disgrace in her native place.
Marten (*turning to* MRS. MARTEN): Tut, tut, wife—Mr. Corder is about to act an honourable part to our child, so cease upbraiding. (*Turning back to* CORDER). When will the wedding take place?

33

Corder : As soon as possible—for tonight we both depart for London.

Marten and Mrs. M. (*out front*): London?

Corder : Yes—for family reasons, our marriage must take place there.

Marten : Why cannot you be married here? Here has she been pointed out in shame. 'Tis here that the stain should be for ever removed from her name.

Mrs. M. (*crossing* MARTEN *to* CORDER): Yes, why cannot she be married at our village church like me and my good husband and let the fiddle be scraping, the bells ringing and all our friends have a jollification?

Corder : I do not wish my mother to know of the marriage till it be over.

Mrs. M. : Very well, William, if Maria wishes to go with you, so be it. (*Turning to* MARTEN). What say you, Father, do you give your consent?

Marten (*crossing to right of* CORDER *and putting his arm around him*): Aye, that I do and willingly. Now, what about some refreshment before you start on your long journey?

Mrs. M. Yes, William do. 'Twill take me but a minute to get it for you.

Corder : Wait! Thank you for your kindness but I must return to the farm at once to fetch my bag—and so farewell.

Mrs. M. : As you wish. (*Moving in to* CORDER *left of* MARTEN). Farewell, son—but how I would have liked to have danced at your wedding. Farewell. (*Exit left*).

Marten : I'll not detain you further for I see you are impatient to depart. Let us hear from you on your arrival in London. Be kind to my child—she has suffered much for you. I now entrust her to you and hope and pray that you will take good care of her.

Corder : Have no fear, I will take care of her all right. (*Aside*). Oh yes, the best possible care.

Marten : God bless you, my son, and as you deal with Maria, so may Heaven deal with you. (*Exit left*).

Corder (*aside*): Heaven? What have I to do with Heaven? The deed I contemplate will close those gates on me for ever. 'Tis Hell must guard me now. *Music Cue 33—(Villain Theme)*. Hence, hence remorse and every thought that's good. The storm that lust began must end in blood (*Exit right*).

End Music Cue 33.

Enter MARIA *left dressed in men's clothes. She is followed by* MRS. MARTEN AND MARTEN.

34

Maria (*crossing right*): Now, dear Mother, I must go.

Mrs. M. (*taking her arm*): Of a sudden, have I a feeling that I do not wish you to go. Last night I had a dream.

Maria : Oh, Mother. (*Starts to cry*),

Mrs. M. (*taking* MARIA *in her arms*): There, child, there—do not cry. You are going to be happy. (*To* MARTEN): Husband, I do not like Maria going. I am terribly afraid some accident will happen to her. I had a dream last night.

Marten : Pooh, pooh — do not tell me of your foolish dreams! The girl will be safe enough. William is a good lad and will protect her. He has his pistol wth him.

Mrs. M. : Pistol! Well—may God protect her! Goodbye, dear child—dear, dear child. (*Kisses her*).

Maria : Goodbye, Mother. (*Starts to move towards exit down right*).

Mrs. M. But once more, dear Maria. (MARIA *returns and* MRS. MARTEN *kisses her again*). Farewell!

Maria : Farewell, Mother, farewell Father. (*Moves to door down right*). But now I must go. (*Returns to kiss* MRS. MARTEN *again*). This must be our last farewell. (*Exit down right*).

Mrs. M. : Our last farewell! May Heaven forbid that it be so.

Music Cue 34—(Link—Maria Theme softly into Villain Theme).

ACT TWO

- SCENE TWO

THE WOOD—*thirty minutes later. Early evening. Enter* CORDER *left*.

Corder (*aside*): A dismal gloom obscures the face of day. Either the sun has slipped behind the clouds or travels down the west of Heaven with more than common speed as if it would avoid the sight of what I now must do. And yet it must be done—there can be no return! Ah, I have forgotten to bring a pickaxe and a spade. *End Music Cue 34.* Fool—thy mind is sore confused! Yet, should I return to fetch them, then might my victim escape. What's to be done? I know—I'll linger here and try to borrow from some passing stranger.

TIM BOBBIN *enters right carrying a pickaxe and a spade. He stops and sits on a tree stump right centre.*

Tim (*aside*): Ah me, I must rest my weary bones awhile, I never get no rest at all. Just as I be going to sit down for half a shake, blow me if old Mr. Marten wasn't at I to dig his garden. But who be this I see here? Why I do believe it be William Corder. (*Aloud—rising*). Hello Mr. Corder!

35

Corder (*to centre stage*): It would appear that you have the advantage of me, fellow.

Tim: What's advantage? I ain't never heard tell of one of them afore. I swear I ain't got one of yours.

Corder (*aside*): A half-wit if ever I saw one. He may serve my purpose well. (*Aloud*). What I mean is that you seem to know me whereas I never clapped eyes on you before.

Tim (*rising*) Know 'ee? That I do—brother-in-law.

Corder: What mean you by brother-in-law?

Tim: I knows all about 'ee. I knows what 'ee be up to, brother-in-law.

Corder (*aside*): Could it be that the fool suspects? I must proceed with caution. (*Aloud*). And what is it that you know all about, fool?

Tim: Ain't 'ee going to marry Maria and ain't I going to marry her sister Nan? So us'll all be one happy family—in a manner of speaking.

Corder (*aside*): What, I a relation of this village idiot? Then am I more than ever determined to rid myself of Maria's shackles. (*Aloud*). Now, fellow, ean you lend me your spade? I will pay you handsomely.

Tim: Why be 'ee wanting a spade—be 'ee going to bury something?

Corder (*aside*): Egad, he does suspect! (*Aloud—fiercely*). What is that you say, boy?

Tim: 'Ee be as fierce as a rat without a tail. I thought maybe that dog of yours had been worrying the sheep and you'd shot him and needed to bury the poor creature.

Corder; No, no! A friend of mine wants me to take a young tree to plant on his estate and I need a spade to dig it up.

Tim: How much will 'ee give I for a pick and spade?

Corder: What do you earn in a day?

Tim: Eighteen pence and they keep I in pudding.

Corder: Then will I give you two shillings for the loan of them. Can you change a five pound note? (*Produces note*).

Tim: Change a five pound note? I never did see one afore in all my life.

Corder: Well then, can you change a sovereign?

Tim: Aye, that I can—if you'll wait till I go to the 'Cat and Fiddle' and get a drink with it.

Corder: No, no—I cannot wait. I'll give you all the change I have and the balance when next we meet.

Tim (*handing over pick and spade*): Here, then you can have the loan of 'em—but just 'ee make sure 'ee lets I have 'em back when 'ee's finished with 'em.

Corder: I'll leave them outside the door of the Red Barn.

36

But now must I be on my way. Here's the money—one shilling piece and two pennies. (*Gives coins and exits left*).

Tim (*aside*): Now then—two shillings he said and here be one shilling and two pence on account. (*Scratches his head*). Now that be—ah yes, I've got it. (*Aloud—calling after* CORDER). And don't 'ee forget 'ee owes I ninepence. I ain't such a fool as can't work that out, I promise 'ee. (*He moves left and looks off*). Dang my buttons, if there ain't a dandy chap kissing my Nan. I'll punch his head till it looks like a pickled cabbage. I'll just step aside and watch 'em. (*Hides right*).

MARIA *enters left followed by* ANNE. MARIA *is dressed as a man.*

Maria (*to centre stage*): Do you think I will be recognised as I cross the fields, Anne?

Anne (*moving left of* MARIA): Not a bit of it. You make a jolly nice little man. I swear that I could almost fall in love with you myself.

Maria: Tell Mother that I will write as soon as I arrive in London. Farewell, dear sister. I must depart, for my William will be waiting. (*They embrace*).

Tim (*aside*): Dang me if I can stand this any longer. (*Moving to D.R.C.—aloud*). Aye, do it again! Her likes it for sure.

Maria (*to* ANNE): Why—it's Tim.

Anne (*aside*): He won't know 'ee dressed the way 'ee be. Let's have a bit of fun, for he's such a coward. (*Takes* MARIA *left and kisses her*).

Tim (*approaching* MARIA): Now then, young feller-me-lad, what be 'ee doing with that young girl?

Anne: He was but asking me—

Tim: You hold your tongue, you shame-faced hussy!

Anne: I never saw the chap before in all my life.

Tim: Oh, what a whopper!

Maria: I'll whop you, my lad, if you dare to address a lady in that manner again.

Tim (*sparring*): All right—come on then—come on!

Maria (*aside to* ANNE): The fellow will kill me.

Anne (*to* MARIA): He's too big a coward. (*To* TIM). If 'ee touch this young man, I'll tear thy eyes out.

Tim: Thee go home or I'll tell thy mother (*Sparring round* MARIA). Come on, come on. I tell 'ee, sir, I demands satisfaction.

Maria (*squaring up to* TIM): You shall have it, sir, and that instantly.

Tim (*aside*): Dang me, this chap'll hurt I. (*Aloud*). I tell 'ee what—as I be of a kind nature, I'll let 'ee off this time.

Anne (*aside to* MARIA): Didn't I say he was a coward?

Maria : Come on, sir, come on I say!

Tim (*crouching down*): Why don't 'ee try hitting someone thy own size?

Maria : I can waste no more time on you. You are a coward, sir. (*To* ANNE). Farewell, sweet, one more kiss. (*They embrace*).

Tim : If 'ee kiss her again, I'll—I'll—I'll—

Maria (*rounding on him*): You'll what, sir?

Tim : I'll—I'll close my eyes. (*Moves up stage with back to audience and puts his hand over his eyes*).

Maria (*to* ANNE): Goodbye, sweet girl, and if this bumpkin annoys you, I'll come from London and I will shoot him through and through. Adieu then, dearest. (*They kiss*). May every bliss be thine till next we meet. (*Aside*). And now for the Red Barn and my dear, dear William (*Exit right*).

Anne (*to centre stage*): He's gone. Oh, Tim, isn't he a nice little man?

Tim (*turning*): Go on false, perfidious one—kissing another chap afore my face. That sort of kissing and cuddling might do for the fine folks in Lunnon but if I has a wife I wants all the kissing and cuddling to myself.

Anne : But I'm not your wife yet.

Tim : No, thee ain't, but thee promised thee would be. Now I finds 'ee to be a false-hearted creature. Oh, I wish I'd smashed that chap.

Anne (*laughing*): No more—I'll tell thee the truth, Tim. That wasn't a man at all. It was my sister, Maria.

Tim : Thy sister Maria! (*Laughs*). Ah, I knows it were her all the time. Do you think as if I wouldn't have smashed him if I'd not known?

Anne : Now then, Tim Bobbin, when are we to get married ?

Tim : I'll put the bungs up at once and go to the blacksmith's and get 'ee a ring.

Anne : A ring like my mother's of finest gimlet gold with a great carbuncle as big as your fist?

Tim (*leading her to the tree stump and sitting her on his lap*): Then us'll retire to a snug little cottage of our own. Then how happy and contented us'll be with a chubby little baby dandlin' on the knee. (*They kiss*).

Anne : But, Tim, what'll folks say—won't they be fair surprised?

Tim : No—not them. I reckons they've guessed—folks is clever.

   Music Cue 35 (*Song*).

38

THOU KNOWS I KNOWS
(TIM AND ANNE)

Tim :   Thou knows I knows thou loves me.
           I knows thou knows I love thee.
           We know
           They know
           We know too
           We love each other like no others do.

Anne :   I knows thou knows I love thee.
           Thou knows I knows thou loves me.
           They know
           We know
           They know too
           No other lovebirds do love like us do.

Tim :   If they know that I love thee
           And they know that thou loves me

Both :   Then we
           Know that
           They know too
           We know we'll marry like true lovers do.

They kiss again.
*Music Cue 36—(Link—Thou Knows into Villain
Theme).*

ACT TWO

SCENE THREE

INTERIOR OF THE RED BARN—*Fifteen minutes later. It is
dimly lit by the light of a single lantern standing on an
upturned box left. Upstage centre are two or three bales
of straw against which are leaning the spade and pickaxe.*
WILLIAM CORDER *is discovered standing right.*
Music Cue 36 continues.

39

Corder : Here is the spot I've fixed on to complete my purpose. Everything is ready to inhume the body. That disposed of, I'll defy detection. I now await my victim. Will she come? (*He looks off right*). Ah yes, for a woman is fool enough to do anything for the man she loves. Who's there? (*Starts back*). Ha, 'tis no one. How foolish are these startling fears. (*Moves to centre stage*). I'll entreat the fiends of hell to work strong within me, drown my fears and slake my thirst for vengeance in her blood! *End Music Cue 36.* Hark, by Heaven, she comes! 'Tis her footsteps bounding across the fields. Little does she think that death is so near. Now, all ye fiends of hell, spur me to the deed—teach me not to feel pity nor remorse. Hand, heart be firm, my reputation save and hurl my victim to an early grave. Hold, she is here! (*Hides up right*).

Music Cue 37—(Maria Theme softly).

Maria (*calling*): William, William—are you here? 'Tis strange he does not answer. (*Moves centre looking for him*). He is not here. (*Moves down left*). How silent is all around. A fearful gloom seems to hang about this place. (*To centre stage*). Oh, William, William, to thee I trust for future happiness! In sweet companionship with thee, I'll sail down life's rough stream 'till death our fond hearts sever. (*Sits on one of the bales*). Here will I await his coming and think of all the happy days life holds in store for me. Such sweet thoughts will dispel the sorrows which now fill my troubled heart.

End Music Cue 37.

Music Cue 38—(Villain Theme).

CORDER *steps out from behind door and moves silently towards* MARIA.

Corder : Maria Marten!

Maria (*rising and moving D.L.C.*): William, is that you? How glad I am to hear your voice, for I have died a hundred times whilst waiting for you in this gloomy spot.

End Music Cue 38.

Corder (*aside*): To die but once will be sufficient for my purpose. (*Aloud*). Were you observed upon the way?

Maria : No, dearest William. Now, let us leave this place, lest we should be seen and recognised by anyone. (*Moving towards exit up right*).

Corder (*crossing to her and catching hold of her*): Stay! Ere we leave this place, we must understand each other.

Maria : What mean you, William? Speak! But speak and ease my tortured breast.

Corder : Listen to me, Maria. But a few days since, you visited the apothecary here in the village did you not?

40

Maria : Why yes, I fetched some lotion for the pain in my old mother's back.

Corder (*twisting her arm roughly*): And did you ask him questions about the medicine I obtained from him for the child?

Maria : I know not what you mean. William, you are hurting me.

Corder : You know exactly what I mean.

Maria : Let us leave at once. My blood is frozen in my veins and I am faint with terror.

Corder : No—not yet, Maria. (*Pulling her roughly towards him*). Tell me—have you told anyone of what you learnt of the apothecary?

Maria : I have not breathed a word to a living soul.

Corder (*pushing her down right but remaining D.R.C.*): Then, by Heaven, thou art in my power and I will keep thee so—aye and for ever!

Music Cue 39—(Maria Theme until Cue 40).

Maria (*aside*): Do I hear aright? My ears must mock me. (*Aloud*). Oh, William, how have I lost thy love?

Corder : Ask thy false heart and it will answer thee.

Maria : No, no, as there is truth in Heaven, I have not wronged thy love. What have I not sacrificed for it?

Corder (*moving to her*): I'll hear no more!

Maria (*kneeling*): Oh, William, behold me on my knees. (*Grasping him*) I pray thee to keep thy promise and make me thy lawful wife. Let me, once again, walk erect and look my fellow creatures in the face, without the blush of shame mantling my cheeks.

Music Cue 40—(Villain Theme).

Corder (*freeing himself from her grasp and moving centre stage*): Marry thee! Mark me, Maria, I brought you here not to marry you, but to let you know my resolution. Instantly swear to keep the murder of the child a secret and renounce all pretensions of becoming my wife or, by Heaven, you never quit this spot alive!

End Music Cue 40.

Maria (*aside*): Oh, wretch! Have I trusted in such a fiend? But no; it cannot be. (*Rising and moving to* CORDER— *aloud*). Oh, William, tell me that you have but sported with me, and I will bless thee.

Corder : Will you take the oath?

Maria : Never, villain, traitor! I will die first!

Corder : Then shall your blood be on your own head.

Music Cue 41—(Villain Theme loudly until Cue 42).

MARIA *trys to escape but* CORDER *seizes her and drags her to the bales of straw.*

Corder : Look behind these bales of straw!

41

Maria : What is it?

Corder : A grave, Maria—a grave! I have dug it with my own hands. Say your prayers, Maria, for you are about to die!

Thunder—Lightning.

Music Cue 42—(Maria Theme).

Maria : But not by your hand—the hand that I have clasped in love and confidence. (*Looking upwards*). Oh, William, think of our little child above. In Heaven it pleads for its mother's life. Oh, spare me, spare me! (*Backs away centre stage*).

End Music Cue 42.

Corder : Will you take the oath? (MARIA *sinks to the ground.* CORDER *moves to upstage of* MARIA). Nay, shrink not, 'tis in vain, for I am desperate in my thoughts and thirst for blood.

Maria : Wretch, since neither prayers nor ears will touch your stony heart, Heaven will surely nerve my arm to to battle for my life. (*She rises and seizes* CORDER).

Music Cue 43—(Villain Theme fast).

Corder : Foolish girl, desist!

Maria : Never with life! (*They struggle*).

Corder : Then die! (*He shoots her*).

MARIA *falls into* CORDER'S *arms.*

Music Cue 44—(Maria Theme softly and slowly until Cue 45).

Maria : William, I am dying. Your cruel hand has stilled the heart that beat in love for thee. Death claims me and with my last breath I die, blessing and forgiving thee. (*She dies*).

Music Cue 45—(Villain Theme slowly until Cue 46).

Corder (*lowering the body to the ground*): Blessing and forgiveness for me, her murderer? What have I done? (*Kneeling beside body*). Oh, Maria, awake, awake— do not look so tenderly upon me! Let indignation lighten from your eye and blast me! (*Rises*). What's that? I thought I heard a woman's voice from out the grave laughing at me. I thought I heard a voice cry 'Vengeance— vengeance is now come in full measure!' (*Moves down left*). Calm thee soul—lie still foul conscience! (*Moves to grave*). I will dispose of the body, deep within this grave. No clue will then remain to risk discovery. All then will be at rest— at rest! (*Moves away to left of bales of straw*). No—no— never at rest—never! never! never! Oh may this crime for ever stand accursed—the last of murders as it is the worst.

Music Cue 46—(Link—Villain Theme into Years That Pass Away).

ACT TWO

SCENE FOUR

THE MARTENS' KITCHEN—*Twelve months later. The upstage area behind the closed traverse curtains, remains set as the Red Barn for the vision sequence which occurs in this scene.* MRS. MARTEN *is seated in the chair left and* MARTEN *in the chair right. He is smoking a pipe. The lamp is lit on the table.*
End Music Cue 46.

Marten : 'Tis strange! Day after day passes and no further tidings of Maria.

Mrs. M. : It is now a full twelve months since she left home and only two letters have we received. The first, from William, saying that she was so taken up with London pleasures she had no time to write, the second in such strange writing, saying she had a gathered hand and could scarce hold the pen. Ah me, I don't feel at all satisfied.

Marten : You look ill, wife. Recent events have robbed you of repose and broken your rest, and remember, wife, we are getting aged now.

Mrs. M. : Yes, Thomas, we are fast declining in the vale of years and soon must be overtaken by death, who hovers o'er our heads ever ready to place his icy fingers on our hearts.

Marten : Yes, wife, and the prayer of the aged parents shall be, as they sink into the silent grave. 'May their last moments on earth be blessed with the tears of their beloved children.'

Mrs. M. : Amen!

(Both rise and meet centre stage for song).
Music Cue 47—(Song).

THE YEARS THAT PASS AWAY
(MR. AND MRS. MARTEN)

43

Mr. M. : Though the years have passed away
And life is nearly o'er,
Mrs. M. : Still my love for you, my dear,
Will last for evermore.
Both : Safe within your heart, my dear,
Forever I will stay
And never, ever need to fear
The years that pass away.
Mr. M. : As long as you are by my side,
I'll face whate'er may be
Mrs. M. : Until, in Heaven we do abide,
Through all eternity.
Both : Safe within your heart, my dear,
Forever I will stay
And never, ever need to fear
The years that pass away.
And never, ever need to fear
The years that pass away.

Encore : *From* 'As long as you' *until end.*

Marten : And now, wife, you need repose. Go sleep for
a while; 'twill drive these sad thoughts from your breast
and recruit your strength. In the meantime, I will make
more enquiries concerning our dear Maria.
Mrs. M. : I will do as you advise me, and may Heaven
bless and comfort us with news of our darling child.
Marten : We will hope for the best. I'll go to the Post
Office and see if there is a letter. Cheer up, wife, rest awhile.
(*To down right*). I'll not be absent long. (*Exit right*).

During the following speech the lights slowly fade so that MRS. MARTEN *is only dimly lit by the light of the single lamp.*

Mrs. M. (*sits in chair left*): A strange drowsiness comes o'er me—a feeling I cannot shake off. It steals upon me and wraps me in its shroud, and were I superstitious I should fear some dire calamity lurked unseen, or death were nigh. Oh. Maria, my thoughts are of thee—Maria, my beloved child I—I. (*She sleeps*).

Music Cue 48—(Maria Theme softly).

The walls fade to show the interior of the Red Barn (this effect can be obtained either by using a painted gauze backing for the kitchen set or by slowly opening the traverse curtains). The lights fade on the kitchen and come up slowly on the Barn. MARIA *enters,* CORDER *comes from up right and after a mimed quarrel, he raises his pistol and shoots her (no sound). He then drags her to the grave, lifts her body and is about to lower it into the grave when* MRS. MARTEN *wakes with a scream. The lights fade on the vision and the single light comes up on the front set.*

End Music Cue 48.

Mrs. M. (*starting up from chair and backing away left*): Help! Help! My child! My child! I saw her—I saw her sure— lifeless and smeared with blood! 'Twas in the Red Barn! And there stood Corder with her poor bleeding body lowering it into a grave. But no, 'twas all a dream! (*Crosses back to chair and leans against it*). Thank God! Thank God, it was but a dream. But how frightful! It has harrowed up my soul with fear. This is the third time that I have dreamed this terrible dream within a week. (*To centre stage*). Oh, Husband! Husband!

MARTEN, TIM *and* ANNE *rush in right,* MARTEN *is carrying a light.*

Marten : Wife, Wife, what has happened?

Anne : Oh, Mother, dear Mother, speak. Oh, my poor dear Mother! (*Crosses to her left and puts her arm around her*).

Marten (*to her right*): What ails thee, wife? How came you to scream so? What has alarmed thee?

Mrs. M. : Oh. husband, I've had such a terrible dream. Maria, my poor child, is murdered.

All : Murdered?

Music Cue 49—(Villain Theme softly).

Mrs. M. : Yes, foully murdered in the Red Barn!

Marten : How know you this?

Mrs. M. : My dream! My dream!

45

Marten : Compose yourself. *End Music cue 49.* Anne, assist your mother to the chair. (*Anne does so and remains standing on her left*—MARTEN *is on her right and* TIM *right centre stage*). Now then, tell us how a mere dream can disturb thee thus.

Mrs. M. : Oh, husband, it was no dream, but the voice of Heaven conveying to a mother's heart the murder of her darling child. This is the third time that I have seen her murdered.

Marten : Tell us exactly what occurred, wife. Dreams are said to be prognostics of some great events, although I find it hard to believe that it is so.

Mrs. M. : I sat myself down in this very chair, over-powered with fatigue, and fell asleep. Methought I saw within the Red Barn, our child, Maria, covered in blood, murdered and stretched on the ground. Beside her stood William Corder with a pistol in his hand. Then, I thought I saw him seize my dear child by the silken handkerchief she wore around her neck and drag her body close to the spot where he had been digging. He was in the act of consigning her body within the horrid grave he had just made when, in my frenzy and horror, I awoke.

Marten (*putting his arm around her shoulder*): Come, wife, banish these timid fancies. Anne, assist and lead your mother to the air. You take one arm and I the other. (*They lift her gently from the chair and take her across right*—TIM *remains centre stage*). Maria, our dear child, will be here tomorrow and then we will—

Mrs. M. (*breaking from them downstage—out to audience*): No! I am not satisfied. I will never rest until I have learnt the fate of my child. (*To* MARTEN). Go, husband, summon the neighbours—fetch more lights and search the barn at once!

Marten : But, wife, I—

Mrs. M. : What, do you hesitate? (*Crossing them to exit right*).
Then, out of it—I'll go myself!

Marten : Very well, wife, I'll go to please you but rest assured all is well with our Maria. I know the heart of Corder well—he is an honest fellow. (*Crossing to* TIM). Come Tim, you'll with me to the Red Barn?

Tim (*backing away left*): You won't catch I going near that barn—oh dear no!

Anne (*moving to right of* MARTEN): Come along, you great coward, or I won't marry 'ee.

Tim : And shall she marry I if I go, Mr. Marten?

Marten : Aye, if she likes thee, I'll give my consent for thou art an honest lad for sure.

Tim : Then I'll go get my pitchfork and stable lantern. (*Exit left*).

Marten : Go, wife, lie thee down.

Anne (*moving to* MRS. MARTEN): I'll go and get thee a cup of green tea. That will settle thy nerves for thee.

Mrs. M. (*at door right*): Oh, husband, husband—hasten, for I feel I cannot rest until this mystery is cleared up. (*Exit with* ANNE *right*).

Enter TIM *from left holding a lantern and pitchfork.*

Marten : Are you ready, Tim? Will you assist a heartbroken father to search for his beloved daughter?

Tim (*moving to right of* MARTEN): Aye—that I will. To the Red Barn! To the Red Barn!

Music Cue 50—(Link 'Hurry' Music into Maria Theme).
MARTEN *and* TIM *hurry off right.*

ACT TWO

SCENE FIVE

INTERIOR OF THE RED BARN—*Thirty Minutes later. The scene opens in darkness except for a shaft of moonlight which shines on the upstage centre area.* MARTEN *enters carrying a lantern.*
End Music Cue 50.

Marten : This is the place. Now then, Tim, I want you to —Tim, where are you, lad? (*Looks off right*). Come on, be not afraid.

Tim (*putting his head round door up right*): I ain't frightened, Mr. Marten—only scared to death (*Withdraws his head*).

Marten : Come along, boy. (*Goes to door and coaxes him in*). Come along, there's no one here—the old barn has not been used for some time. (*Moves to below bales of straw with* TIM *on his right*).

Tim : That be true. 'Tis twelve months since I was here last. 'Twas two or three days after Maria went off with that William Corder, I comes for my pick and spade, but they had been putting loads of hay in the third bay and I reckon as how they must have buried 'em for, search as I would, I could not find no trace of 'em.

Marten : What's that you say—your pick and spade? What were your pick and spade doing in the Red Barn?

Tim : Why dang me, didn't I lend 'em to this William Corder the very night they went off together to Lunnon and didn't he promise to pay I ninepence when he saw I again? And has he not cheated I of my ninepence, for I have seen nor it nor he since that very night?

47

Marten : Enough of your trifling pence, you foolish lad; do you not see what dreadful thing this could mean?

Tim : Aye, that I do—that he's a thief and I have lost my ninepence.

Marten : Heaven grant that's all he be—Heaven grant it!

Tim (*starting back*): Oh, look, Mr. Marten, look! (*Pointing up stage left*).

Marten : What, boy, what do you see?

Tim : A ghost, Mr. Marten—I saw a ghost!

Marten (*moving up to behind straw and kicking it*). 'Twas but a rat—this old barn is full of them. Come, Tim, hold the light.

Tim (*moving to right of* MARTEN *to take the light*): All right, Mr. Marten.

Marten (*bending down and moving some of the straw*): There's something here—hold the light nearer, Tim. Be not afraid.

Tim (*shaking so that the light bobs up and down*): I ain't afraid, Mr. Marten—my nerves is as steady as a rock.

Marten : It's a pick.

Tim : My pick for sure!

Marten (*moving some more straw*): And here's your spade.

Tim : Yes, tis mine—I'd swear to it.

Marten (*examining spade*): What's this — here on the spade?

Tim : (*bending over and examining it*): Why dang me—'tis a stain that looks for all the world like blood.

Marten : It is—it is and here on the handle—do you not see—human hairs, long hairs from a woman's head?

Tim (*rising and moving away right*): Oh, I wish I'd got my ninepence.

Marten : Bring the light back—bring it back! Something seems to tell me that my poor wife's dream is only too true.

Tim (*moving to right of* MARTEN *and bending down to pick something up*). Oh look, Mr. Marten, here's a young pup of a gun!

Marten (*rising and moving to* TIM *to take gun*): A pistol! The name? (*Examines it*). William Corder! Search, Tim, search; I feel we are about to discover some awful crime.

They move about behind straw and examine the ground closely.

Marten : Ah, the ground has been moved here. Dig, Tim, dig! Here, give me the light. (*Takes it and kneels while* TIM *gets the spade*).

Tim : I will, Mr. Marten, but don't leave me. (*Starts to dig*).

Marten (*bending close to spot*). What's this? A necktie! 'Tis Maria's—many a time have I seen her wearing it. Dig, Tim, dig!

Tim : I will, Mr. Marten, I will—oh Lordy me, Lordy me!

Marten : What is it?

Tim (*rising and backing away left with spade*): Murder! Murder ! ! !

Marten : Oh' it's true—it's true! Our daughter has been murdered—basely done to death by that William Corder!

Enter MRS. MARTEN *and* ANNE *up right.*

Marten (*rising and standing between them and the grave*): No, wife, away! You must not set foot in this awful place.

Mrs. M. (*moving to* MARTEN). I could not wait there in the cottage. I had to come to find what news there be. I had to follow you.

Anne : I pleaded with her not to come but 'twas of no avail.

Marten : Better she had been spared the sight of the murdered body of our poor daughter that is no more.

Mrs. M. : Then 'tis true! But no—it cannot be 'twas but a dream.

Marten : No dream—alas, no dream. Anne, take your mother from this dreadful spot.

ANNE *takes* MRS. MARTEN *right and comforts her as she weeps.*

Anne : Now, Mother, now. Come, hush now, hush!

Marten : Oh my poor murdered child! (*Moves to down centre*). But justice now must take the place of tears. For if in England, justice be not dead, the villain for this deed shall lose his head!.

Anne (*moving to* MARTEN): Dear Father, do not upset yourself so.

Marten : My poor Maria—the child of all I loved the most, now torn from my arms for ever.

Anne : Hold, dear Father, you have a daughter who will make you happy yet.

Tim (*moving to left of* MARTEN): Aye, and a son that is to be.

Marten : She was the darling, the pride of my heart, the hope, the sunlight of my life. *Music Cue 51—(Maria Theme softly)*. Oh how happy was I once. My honest English fireside, circled with my little family—all joyous, all content. I thought the evening of my life should set in peace— but a villain—has blasted all my hopes, robbed me of my child and savagely murdered her.

End Music Cue 51.

Mrs. M. : Oh, Heaven support me! (*Starts to faint*).

Anne (*moving quickly to* MRS. MARTEN *and catching her*). Mother, dear Mother! Alas! Alas!

49

Marten (*kneeling*): Great God, let thy just vengeance light upon this monster. Deliver him into the hands of justice—show no mercy for the bloody deed.

Tim (*lifting him up*): Mr. Marten, do not go on so.

Marten : I took him to my arms, fostered him, called him my son and as he led my poor Maria from my humble roof, I cried 'Heaven bless thee.' I gave the murderer of my child a poor old father's blessing. Oh, Heaven shield me or I shall go mad. (*Crosses* TIM *to down left*).

Tim (*moving down to* MARTEN). Me and Anne will comfort you, Mr. Marten.

Marten : I know it, Tim, but my poor Maria—I see her now before my eyes, mangled and bleeding, pointing to her gory wounds. She beckons me! (*Rushes to grave and kneels left of it*). Thy father's here, thy father's here! I seem to hear her cry for vengeance from the grave (*Rising*). I will revenge thee, child! I will revenge thee! (*Rushes off up right*).

Mrs. M. : Come, Anne, let us follow him lest in his frenzy he may commit some rash act that will add to our sorrows. (*They exit up right*).

Tim (*alone—calling*). Don't leave me, Mrs. Marten—Anne, Anne I'll take care of thee! (*Rushes to door, checks and turns to face out to declaim*): And if, in England, justice be of use, this deed shall then cook Corder's goose! (*Suddenly sees grave again*). Anne! (*Runs to door*). Mrs. Marten, wait for me, wait for me!.

Music Cue 52—(Link—'Thou Knows fast into One and One).

ACT TWO

SCENE SIX

THE WOOD—*A month later. Bird song is heard. Enter* TIM *and* ANNE *from right.*

Tim : Now come 'ee sit down on this old tree stump for I've a wonderous thing to show 'ee.

Anne (*sitting*): Come on then quick, for I cannot wait to find out what 'tis you've dragged me all this weary way to see.

Tim : Very well, but first 'ee must close thy eyes tight.

Anne (*closing eyes*): I've closed them.

Tim : And no peeping, mind. (*To left of Anne*). Now then. (*Produces box from behind his back*). Hold out thy hands. (*She does so*). Here it be—and first 'ee must guess what 'tis and then can 'ee open your eyes.

50

Anne (*feeling box*): 'Tis a box—a little box. What be in it?

Tim : Can 'ee not guess?

Anne :—No, stop your nattering, thou old fool, and let I open my eyes.

Tim : Old fool indeed! And after I bought 'ee a ring of bright candlestick gold.

Anne : A ring!

Tim : Dang it, now I've told 'ee what it was. A nice bright yellow one it is too when I rubs it on my breeches.

Anne : Can I look now?

Tim : Thou can open thy eyes but 'ee is not to look inside the box yet—bide thy time. First I must tell 'ee. I went to blacksmith's for it. Says he 'What does 'ee want a ring for?' 'To get married in,' says I. 'Get along,' says he, 'I only put rings through pigs' noses.' So I went to a jeweller's shop and asked him for a ring to get married, with a big carbuncle on, like 'ee said.

Anne : And did you get one?

Tim : Nay, for the chap said it must be a plain one to get married with.

Anne : Oh, do let I look at it, my mouth waters to see it.

Tim : Very well then—open the box.

Anne (*opening box and taking out ring*): Oh, what a beauty! (*Trys to put it on*). But it be too big!

Tim : Then put it on thy thumb.

Anne : You don't put wedding rings on thy thumb.

Tim : Then must 'ee wear it on thy wedding finger and hope that it will shrink to the proper size when 'ee puts it in the wash tub. Well 'ee's got the ring, so I'm off to parson's to get wed. (*Starts to go off left*).

Anne (*getting up and running after him*): Stop! Stop! You cannot get married without I.

Tim (*stopping and turning to* ANNE): What, do it take two of we to get wed?

Anne : Of course, you stupid lad—us goes in church two and us comes out one.

Tim (*scratching his head*): Well, dang my buttons, how do they do that? In two and come out one? Why that be conjuring. Be us both rolled into one then? Blow the whiskers off the eyes of my grandmother's sister's aunt's tom. cat if ever I heard of such a thing in all my life.

Music Cue 53—(Song).

51

ONE AND ONE MAKES ONE
(TIM *and* ANNE)

Both : When we went to village school,
Even then the simplest fool
Learned that one and one makes two.
Sums like that ain't hard to do.
Anne : But I tells thee when we're wed,
That the answer's one instead.
Tim : I may not be very bright
But I knows that can't be right.
Anne : One and one makes one, I say
On our happy wedding day.
Tim : But I'll prove to you ere long
That you're very, very wrong.
Anne : One and one makes one, 'tis true.
Parson will unite us two.
Tim : When we's wed then I tell thee
One and one will soon make—three.

Music Cue 54—(Link—One and One into London Town).

ACT TWO

SCENE SEVEN

INTERIOR OF CORDER'S HOUSE AT BRENTFORD—*A week later. There is a table left centre, with a chair behind it and another to the right of it, in which* CORDER *is seated. End Music Cue 54.*

Corder : How strange is every action of my life. I met by chance a lady sometime ago at Seaford, where I had been for the recovery of my health. From thence, I came to London. We parted and, wonderful to say, she was one of the women who answered my advertisement for a wife. Now am I married to her and, being a wealthy and accomplished lady, all things now proceed in my favour. (*Rises*). I'll call the servant and see if there are any letters. (*Moves to stage right to ring the bell and returns to table and sis in chair above it*).

ALICE RUMBLE, *the maid, enters right.*

Alice : You rang for me, sir ?

52

Corder : Are there any letters, Alice?

Alice : No, sir—only one for the mistress and that I have taken to her room.

Corder : The mistress is in her room?

Alice : Yes, sir, she complained of a headache and is lying down.

Corder : Come here, Alice.

Alice (*moving to right of* CORDER): Yes, sir?

Corder (*pinching her cheek*): You are a comely wench, are you not? (*Catching hold of her and pulling her onto his knee*). Stay for a while and keep me company. I vow that since my wife turned this house into a school, I see her but rarely. (*Tries to kiss her*).

Alice (*struggling to get away*): Nay, sir, I have work to do and 'tis not proper that you should use me so.

Corder : Egad, I'd treat thee well enough if you'd but say the word.

Alice (*freeing herself and getting up*): No, sir, please!

Corder : Very well—but think on what I have said.

Alice : Can I go now, sir? (*Moving towards exit*).

Corder : One minute—why did you not come when I rang for you half an hour ago?

Alice : I was looking out of the window, watching a poor man go by to execution.

Music Cue 55—(London Town slowly).

CORDER *appears distraught.*

Corder : Execution? What has he done?

Alice : Oh, he's murdered some poor girl. Lor bless me, sir, you've got a face like a ghost.

Corder (*rising*): Leave the room at once!

End Music Cue 55.

Alice : Yes, sir, certainly, sir. (*Rushes off right*).

Corder (*aside*): Now are my days as haunted as my nights. Last night, my rest was disturbed by a horrid, distressful dream. I saw Maria Marten's form, arrayed in white, wandering along the fields. Twice did she seem to pause and cast her eyes towards the Red Barn. I saw no more. 'Tis said that dreams oft denote some hidden truth. (*To centre stage*). But no; she sleeps for ever and dreams are but the fleeting visions of a troubled mind—no more.

Music Cue 56—(Gypsy Theme).

Enter ALICE *right.*

Corder : What is it?

Alice : There is a man here says he must speak with you.

Corder : Who is he?

Alice : I have never seen him before, sir. He is a stranger.

Corder (*aside*). A stranger enquiring for me. (*Aloud*). I don't feel in the mood to see visitors. Tell the gentleman I am not at home.

End Music Cue 56.

Alice (*calling off right*): Master says he's not at home!

Corder: You blockhead! Get out!

Exit ALICE *right.* PHAROS LEE *enters right and moves to right of* CORDER.

Corder (*agitated*): Were you enquiring for me, sir?

Lee (*first looking at* CORDER *closely*): Is your name William Corder?

Corder: My name is Corder, sir. What pray is your business with me?

Lee (*slowly and distinctly*): Of a very serious nature, Mr. Corder.

Corder (*with great uneasiness*): Serious?

Lee: Yes, indeed. You formerly lived in Polstead, Suffolk?

Corder: That is my native place, but I have not been there for some time.

Lee: You had an old barn on your property, known as the Red Barn?

Corder (*moving away D.L.C.—aside*). Who is this man? What knowledge has he of the happening in the Red Barn? (*Aloud*). Yes, quite true— I do recall a barn to which I believe the local people gave that name—what of it?

Lee (*moving to right of* CORDER *before speaking*): Have you ever known a young woman named Maria Marten?

Corder: Never! Never! You must be mistaken, certainly you must. I am not the person you are searching for.

Lee: I do not think I am mistaken. You surely must recollect a girl of that name.

Corder: No, no! I have never known anyone by that name. I tell you—you are mistaken.

Lee: Now, William Corder, I have asked you twice, I shall ask you a third time. Did you ever know a young woman of the name of Maria Marten?

Corder: Oh, yes—now I remember—my brother introduced me at one of the village merrymakings, when I was down from London.

Lee: My name is Lee. I am a Bow Street Officer. It is my duty to tell you that I arrest you on a charge of murder.

Music Cue 57--(Villain Theme).

CORDER *starts back.* LEE *moves to him, places his hand on his shoulder and shows him some handcuffs.*

Corder: Murder—what murder?

Lee: The murder of Maria Marten.

Corder: Murder? Me? Oh, impossible—it cannot be!

Lee (*moving centre*): Her body has been found.
End Music Cue 57.
Corder: But even if her body has been found in the Red Barn what is that to do with me?
Lee (*turning*): I did not say where her body had been found.
Corder (*aside*). Ah, I have trapped myself. (*Aloud*). What I meant to say was—.
Lee: Enough! You have partly confessed your crime. You are my prisoner! (*Moves to* CORDER). I must search you, sir. (*Puts his hand into* CORDER'*s pocket and produces a pistol*). A pistol! (*Examines it and pulls the trigger. It fires*). Loaded! 'Tis the fellow to the one found in the Red Barn. William Corder—this is not the only crime for which you will have to answer in Heaven.
Corder: What mean you?
Music Cue 58—(Gypsy Theme).
Lee: Think of the poor gypsy woman you shot down.
Corder: What know you of that?
Lee: I knew well the woman you murdered.
Corder: Murdered?
Lee: Aye, murdered. You shot her down to seal her lips on some terrible secret she held of yours. You had wronged her by betraying her sister and driving her brother away to a foreign land. (*To centre stage*). I am that brother! *End Music Cue 58.* I took the oath of vengeance on my sister's grave and swore that I would hunt you down. I joined the Law to complete the task. You are a prisoner within my hands at last—my vengeance is fulfilled! And now, Corder, it is necessary that you accompany me.
Corder (*moving to left of* LEE): I beseech you to grant me but one favour.
Lee: If it be within reason.
Corder: Lest this alarm my family, will you say that I have been arrested for debt?
Lee: I will do so. And now you must come with me to Lambeth Police Office in order to answer the complaint preferred against you by the magistrates assembled there.
Corder: Sir, I am ready but, as the morning is cold, may I be allowed to fetch my coat from yonder room? (*Indicates left*).
Lee: You can do so.
Corder (*moving to door left*): Thank you. (*Aside*). By the window will I escape. (*Exit left*).

LEE *goes to door left, sees something and rushes off left blowing a whistle. Music Cue 59—(Chase Music).* CORDER *enters up left and runs across right, pursued by* LEE. *He runs off right, followed by* LEE. LEE *re-enters*

55

down right with CORDER *following.* LEE *turns and catches* CORDER.

Lee : So, you would escape me! (*Drags* CORDER *to centre stage*). Villain, I would have treated you like a gentleman. Now shall I treat you as a common felon—come!

Corder : Fate, fate—thou has indeed caught me. Now am I truly lost, lost!

Music Cue 59 ends.

Music Cue 60—(Villain Theme slowly into Ballad of William Corder slowly).

ACT TWO

SCENE EIGHT

THE CONDEMNED CELL—*Several weeks later. The only furniture—a bench left centre with a small table to the left of it. There is a lamp burning on the table on which there is also paper, pen and ink.* CORDER *is centre stage.*

Corder : So ends my dream of wealth. Life's fleeting dream is closing fast, and the great conflict, 'gainst which I warred with Heaven and man, is now upon the wane. *End Music Cue 60.* I have been tried, condemned and today am I to meet the hangman. (*Moving to bench*). Hundreds are now flocking to see me suspended between Heaven and earth. (*Sits on bench*). Since my trial, night after night have I tried to sleep but 'twas denied me. But now, when sleep eternal approaches in the form of death, my eyes grow weary and my eyelids close on the world of misery and thought.

Music Cue 61—(Maria Theme slowly).

His head drops—He falls asleep. MARIA's *spirit appears right.*

Maria : William, look on the murdered form of the girl who loved you. The last dread act of justice is about to be dealt upon thee. Look on thy sinless victim, who in life adored thee, now wandering here unearthly, pale and cold. (*To centre stage*). See! See from whence her life blood gushed. You thought to escape the power of justice but the all-seeing eye was on your every action. Farewell, William, farewell. (*Starts to back away right*). Thy poor Maria pities and forgives thee. (*She is now by exit right*). Farewell, William, fear not—I shall be with you on the scaffold. (*Exit right*).

End Music Cue 61.

Corder (*to centre stage*): Away! Mercy, pardon, pity spare me! 'Tis gone—a dream! 'Tis but the darkness of my soul that haunts me thus.

56

Enter LEE *right.*

Lee : Prisoner, the hour of your execution is at hand but an old man wishes to speak with you.

Corder : Who is it?

Lee : The father of your victim—Thomas Marten.

Corder : I will not see him (*Aside*). And yet, might the world brand me a coward. (*Aloud*). Wait! Admit him.

Exit LEE *right.*

Corder (*Aside*): Courage, William, courage—for now, as never before, do you require all your nerve.

Enter MARTEN *right. He crosses to* CORDER *centre stage.*

Marten : William, think not I come to upbraid you in your last moments, though it was a cruel act to ruin my poor child and then to murder her. But now you are about to take the long journey into the valley of death, a doubt is on my mind. Tell me, truly—did you kill my poor child?

Corder : No, no, I swear it was circumstancial evidence they convicted me on. (*Moving down left*). I am innocent—innocent!

Marten : Then, Heaven have mercy on them that have condemned thee. But be you innocent or guilty, I come not to triumph. I pity and forgive thee, whatever you may have done. (*Moves to* CORDER *and puts his hand on his shoulder*).

Corder (*without turning*): Pity and forgiveness from you?

Marten : Yes, William, and may Heaven forgive you too.

Corder (*turning to* MARTEN): Mr. Marten, your words have touched my heart. I will confess to you what I have denied to my judge. Yes—I did kill Maria. And from that moment have I known no rest. Just now, as I slept, I thought she came to me, not as I saw her last in death at my feet but in all her radiant beauty. Then methought she spoke to me, crying out that she would be with me on the scaffold and that she forgave and pitied me.

Marten : William, I would not have thy conscience for all the gold the world could give. (*Moving to centre stage*). Repent, ere it be too late! (*Turning*). Farewell, William—and Heaven have mercy on your soul. (*Exit right*).

Corder : Farewell—and Heaven bless you for your forgiveness. Guilt, guilt I cannot hide thee! (*Rushes to table and writes rapidly*). Lee! (*rushes to right*). Pharos Lee!

Enter LEE *right.*

Lee : What is it?

Corder (*pushing a paper into* LEE'S *hand*): There is my confession. I am the murderer of Maria Marten!

Lee : Then justice hath fulfilled her sacred office to the bent.

57

Corder : She hath! She hath! Guilt—crime—horror—all is there!

Lee : The world shall hear of this.

Corder : I am guilty of the crime. May Heaven have mercy on my soul!

A bell begins to toll slowly.

Lee : Come, the hour of execution has arrived.

Corder : I am ready; my course is finished. *Music Cue 62— (Ballad slowly until Cue 63).* May innocence and virtue pray for the peace of my departing soul! My span of life was short and few my days, yet count my crimes for years and I have lived a century. Thus justice, in compassion to mankind, cuts off a wretch like me, and may my example secure countless thousands from a similar ruin. (*Falls on his knees*). When murder stains a soul with a fearful dye, then blood for blood is nature's dreadful cry.

The backing dissolves (or traverse curtains draw back) to show the assembled cast grouped on the stage. CORDER *remains down centre.*

Music Cue 63—(Song).

THE BALLAD OF WILLIAM CORDER

All : His name was William Corder, to you we do declare.
He courted Maria Marten, most beautiful and fair.

Corder : I promised I would marry her upon a certain day,
Instead of which I was resolved to take her life away.

All : He went to fetch his gun then, a pickaxe and a spade,
He went into the Red Barn and there he dug her grave.

58

Maria :	With heart so light, I thought no harm, to meet him I did go.
All :	He murdered her all in the barn and laid her body low.
	Her mother's nights disturbed were and she dreamed three nights o'er
Mrs. Marten:	My daughter I saw murdered upon the Red Barn floor.
	I sent my husband to the barn, where in the ground he thrust
Mr. Marten :	And there I found my daughter dear amingling with the dust.
All :	And there he found his daughter dear amingling with the dust.
Corder :	Adieu, my loving friends, now my glass is nearly run.
	The dreaded hour has come and my life is almost done.
	So you young men that do pass by, be warned by what you see

A hangman's noose is lowered to above CORDER'S *head.*

	For murdering Maria they'll hang me on a tree.
All :	For murdering Maria they'll hang him on a tree.

CORDER *steps into the line for the CURTAIN CALL.*

THE QUEEN

Marten : Three cheers for Her Majesty!
After the cheers, the cast start to pack up the props, etc., whilst the audience are going out. MR. MARTEN *makes an announcement 'Next week, Upton Snodsbury Empire' (or what have you.) The cast drift off, in ones or twos, through the auditorium or into the wings.*

PRODUCTION NOTES

STYLE OF PERFORMANCE

The difficulty we encounter when we set about producing a melodrama is that, whereas we understand that the less sophisticated audiences of the 19th century accepted them with a fair measure of credulity, it would be almost impossible to expect a modern audience to take them seriously. How then should a producer tackle them for presentation today?

The first solution might appear to be to burlesque them unmercifully. I do not agree with this method of approach. This style of presentation might work for a short extract, but for a full evening's entertainment the joke wears thin very quickly. I have found that the most successful way is to overplay them—that is to say, to use the style of acting we now label 'ham' and to very slightly burlesque those passages where the dialogue is too absurd to be treated in any other manner. But it is very important to remember that the audience must never be aware that you are laughing at the characters being portrayed. It is the high seriousness of the play which causes hilarity. Another thing to look out for is the juxtaposition of overstatement with understatement which should get good laughs.

Movement and gesture should be exaggerated rather like the old silent films. A convention of melodrama rarely used in the modern play is the aside. There are several ways of treating this, but boldness should be the key. The aside given in a stage whisper, with the back of the hand shielding the actor's mouth from the other players can be amusing and can be used occasionally, but by far the most laughs are achieved by the actor who breaks away from the characters to whom he is speaking and approaches the footlights and addresses the audience directly while everyone else on stage 'freezes' for the duration of the aside, in whatever position they are in at the time. Situations like this occur throughout the play, and the more ridiculous the position the actors are left in during the 'freeze,' the funnier it is.

The temptation to play melodrama slowly must be avoided at all cost. There should be a good overall pace so that the audience are not allowed to realise how absurd the situation is before they are whisked on to the next improbability.

As with other melodramas played today, audience participation is essential and should be encouraged by every possible means.

To sum up, I would say—paint the scenes boldly with broad strokes, exaggerate, caricature, and do not be afraid of overstatement. To the actor I would say that if you underplay you may be certain that the audience will laugh at you rather than at the character you are portraying, but if you play the part with all the stops out, if you treat this as that unique opportunity to overact almost unreservedly, then not only will you enjoy yourself, but you may be sure that the audience will, too.

SETTINGS

This version of 'Maria Marten' has been so designed that alternate scenes can be played in front of traverse curtains thus reducing the time taken to effect a scene change. All the settings are very simple and as all the entrances and exits are from left or right, back drops could be used for all the full-stage settings and, if, required, in place of the suggested traverse curtains for the front stage scenes.

60

The two 'grave' scenes have been arranged in such a way that the graves are not seen by the audience. This obviates the difficulty of stage traps.

The setting of the last scene, in the condemned cell, is a simple cut-out of prison bars set between half-opened traverse curtains. At the end of the play, as the traverse curtains open to reveal the assembled cast, the cut-out is slid away.

There are, of course, many other ways in which the play could be staged, but the keynote should always be simplicity as it is essential that there are no waits between scenes.

FURNITURE AND PROPERTIES

A full list of the furniture and properties referred to in the script appears at the end of this script. Producers may, of course, wish to add items of stage dressing to these, but if the set changes are to be effected swiftly these are best kept to a minimum in this type of play.

MUSIC

The melodies of the twelve songs are printed with the lyrics in the main text of the book. In addition, every music cue is given in detail in the text at the point it occurs.

The play may be performed without songs if required but they are not difficult and add much to the spirit of the show. The ability to 'put a song over' is more important thant a good singing voice. If the songs are sung with panache, an audience is less likely to notice that a singer may be rather inexperienced.

However, even if it is decided to omit the songs in whole or part, 'mood' music is essential. The full piano score includes themes for villain, heroine, etc., as well as the full arrangements for the songs. Copies may be purchased from the publishers of the play. The link music between scenes is intended only to cover the scene changes and should end as soon as the next scene is ready, except where indicated in the music plot. Often it will be possible to play only a few bars between scenes.

In the production at the Swan Theatre, a drummer was used throughout the show with great success. Not only did he accompany the comedy songs but provided the thunder, footsteps, drum rolls, etc.

'The Years that Pass Away' is the show-stopper if presented in the following manner. Mr. Marten sings the first two lines straight but after that Mrs. Marten sings hers as though she were a Victorian prima donna, with lots of voice and gestures.

After visually communicating to the audience 'she's at it again,' he attempts to restrain her for the rest of the song but, on the last two lines decides 'if you can't beat 'em, join 'em.'

The encore is sung very quietly, with heads together until the last two lines when both characters sing fortissimo.

Comedy dances for in between the verses of the Tim and Anne songs are very effective.

It must be pointed out that no alteration or addition to the music, except by way of transposition or arrangement for additional instruments, may be made without the prior permission of the publishers, who are unlikely to grant such permission except in very special circumstances. Permission is not required to omit one or more of the songs.

COSTUME AND MAKE-UP

The period of the play is early 19th century but it is suggested that the costumes need not be too accurate. The 'rustics' should look very much so and the villain the traditional top-hatted, dyed-in-the-wool villain of melodrama. Make-up should also be exaggerated.

LIGHTING

A simplified lighting plot appears following these notes. Where there are facilities for follow spots, additional cues will be necessary. For example, it is very effective during the songs, to take the stage lighting to half and cover the singers by follow spots, cross-fading at the end of the song. A green follow spot on Corder on some of his entrances and soliloquies adds much to the atmosphere. If it is possible to put in old-fashioned footlights, these also help to re-create the Victorian theatre. Old dried-milk or oil tins, cut in half, and painted black make very good imitations of the old cowl type floats.

CASTING

This should not present any difficulties as this play has a pre-ponderance of female roles. For companies with limited numbers, the parts of Johnny and Lee might be doubled as might Petra, Rosa and Carmen with Alice, Meg and Anne. In the production at the Swan Theatre, all the female members of the cast, except Maria, played gypsies and all the gypsies, except Nell played villagers in the opening scenes.

If it appears that Anne and Maria are unlike in their manner of speech, although sisters, this is, of course, so. At the time when the first versions of this play were presented, characters were all stock types. Thus Maria is the 'heroine' and Anne the comedy character, described on contemporary programmes, as 'chambermaid.' By the same token Marten is the 'heavy father,' Mrs. Marten the 'character old woman,' Tim Bobbin the 1st low comedian' and so on. Oddly this play does not include that traditional character beloved of Victorian audiences—the hero.

LIGHTING PLOT

PROLOGUE
Working lights until cue 1.
ACT I—SCENE I
1. To open:—Sunlit exterior.
2. During song 'Love at last':—Slow fade to twilight.
3. End of scene:—Fade to blackout.
ACT I—SCENE II
4. To open:—Moonlit exterior.
5. End of scene:—Fade to blackout.
ACT I—SCENE III
6. To open:—Sunlit exterior.
7. Exit of Corder (page 25) Lightning.
8. End of scene:—Fade to blackout.
ACT I—SCENE IV
9. To open:—Moonlit exterior.
10. End of scene:—Fade to blackout.
ACT I—SCENE V
11. To open:—Interior evening.
12. End of scene:—Fade to blackout.
ACT I—SCENE VI
13. To open:—Moonlit exterior.
14. During song 'A Gypsy Lament':—Fade stage, cover gypsies with spot. At the end of the song, bring up red glow offstage left.
15. End of scene:—Slow fade to blackout.

INTERVAL
ACT II—SCENE I
16. To open:—Interior daylight.
17. End of scene:—Fade to blackout.
ACT II—SCENE II
18. To open:—Exterior, early evening.
19. End of scene:—Fade to blackout.
ACT II—SCENE III
20. To open:—Dimly lit interior. Lamp lit.
21. Corder:—You are about to die (page 52); Lightning.
22. End of scene:—Fade to blackout.
ACT II—SCENE IV
23. To open:—Interior evening. Lamp D.L.C. lit.
24. Exit of Marten (page 55). Start very slow fade of D.S. area and bring up U.S. barn area.
25. End of Corder and Maria mime (page 55) as Mrs. Marten screams fade U.S. and bring in D.S. area.
26. Entrance of Marten (page 55) bring up lighting to back up lantern.
27. End of scene:—Fade to blackout.
ACT II—SCENE V
28. To open:—Dimly lit interior; shaft of moonlight on U.S.C. area.
29. Entrance of Marten (page 57) increase lighting.
30. End of scene:—Fade to blackout.
ACT II—SCENE VI
31. To open:—Daylight exterior.
32. End of song 'One and One makes One.' Snap blackout.
ACT II—SCENE VII
33. To open:—Daylight interior.
34. End of scene:—Fade to blackout.
ACT II—SCENE VIII

63

35. To open:—Dimly lit interior; backing for lamp left.
36. As Corder falls asleep (page 66), cross fade main lighting with light on ghost of Maria R.C. An ultra violet lamp can be used here.
38. As bell beings to toll (page 68). Cross fade D.S. area with U.S. area leaving a spot on Corder D.S.C.
39. Curtain call—Full lighting.

FURNITURE AND PROPERTY PLOT

Only the properties and furniture referred to in the script are listed here—stage dressing, etc., can, of course, be added at the discretion of the producer.

PROLOGUE
Prop basket, Costumes, Scarves, Scripts, Mirror, Make-up.

ACT I—SCENE I
On stage: Maypole (centre stage).
Bench (right of cottage door).
Bench (around tree right).
Off stage: Mug of water.
Pole with mask and sheet.

ACT I—SCENE II
Personal: CORDER: Two coins.

ACT I—SCENE III
Personal: CORDER: White hat, silver-topped cane.
On stage: As Scene I except maypole.

ACT I—SCENE IV
Personal: NELL: Bottle of poison.
CORDER: Purse of money.
On stage: Tree stump right.

ACT I—SCENE V
Personal: CORDER: Bottle of poison.
On stage: Table U.S.C.
2 chairs (above and left of table).
Cradle D.S.R.
Spoon on table.

ACT I—SCENE VI
Personal: MARIA: Bundle.
CORDER: Spade. Pistol (loaded).
On stage: Small hillock (centre stage).
Small stick.

ACT II—SCENE I
CORDER: Bag containing male clothes.
Pistol.
On stage: 2 armchairs.
Small table with lamp on it.

ACT II—SCENE II
Personal: TIM: Pickaxe. Spade.
CORDER: Coins and five pound note.
MARIA: Carpet bag.
On stage: Tree stump R.C.

64

ACT II—SCENE III

Personal: CORDER: Pistol (loaded).
On stage: Two or three bales of straw piled U.S.C.
              Upturned box D.L.C.
              Lamp on box.

ACT II—SCENE IV

Personal: MARTEN: Pipe.
              CORDER: Pistol.
              TIM: Lantern. Pickaxe.
Off stage: Lantern.
              Pitchfork.
Upstage set as for Act II Scene III.

ACT II—SCENE V

On stage: Same as barn setting in previous scene.
              With the addition of : —
              Spade pick and pistol behind straw.
              TIM: Lantern. Pitchfork.
              MARTEN: Lantern.

ACT II—SCENE VI

Personal: TIM: Ring in box.
On stage: Tree stump right.

ACT II—SCENE VII

Personal: LEE: Handcuffs. Police whistle.
              CORDER: Pistol.
On stage: Table L.C.
              2 chairs above and left of table.
              Bell pull right.

ACT II—SCENE VIII

Personal: LEE: Keys.
On stage: Bench L.C.
              Small table left.
              Paper, pen and ink on table.
              Hangman's noose (suspended above stage to be
              lowered on cue).